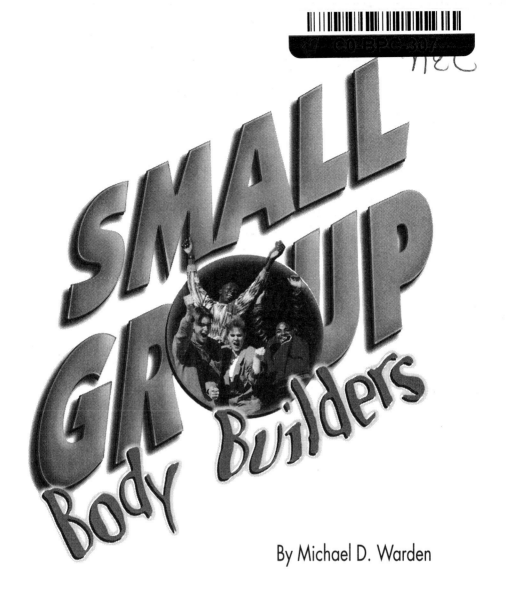

SMALL GROUP
GROUP
Body Builders

By Michael D. Warden

Group

Loveland, Colorado

SMALL-GROUP **BODY BUILDERS**

Copyright © 1998 Michael D. Warden

Small-Group Body Builders is a revised version of the previously published book *Small Church Youth Ministry Programming Ideas.*

Credits
Editors: Steve Parolini and Amy Simpson
Creative Development Editor: Paul Woods
Chief Creative Officer: Joani Schultz
Copy Editor: Pamela Shoup
Art Director: Randy Kady
Cover Art Director: Jeff A. Storm
Cover Designer: Becky Hawley
Computer Graphic Artist: Randy Kady
Cover Photo: @CLEO Photography
Production Manager: Gingar Kunkel

Library of Congress Cataloging-in-Publication Data

Warden, Michael D.
    Small-group body builders / by Michael D. Warden
      p.   cm.
    Rev. ed of: Small church youth ministry programming. 1994.
    Includes bibliographical references.
    ISBN 0-7644-2049-6
    1. Church group work with teenagers. I. Warden, Michael D.
Small church youth ministry programming. II. Title.
    BV4447.W37 1998
    259'.23--dc21   97-41218
                                                 CIP

10 9 8 7 6 5 4 3 2 1   07 06 05 04 03 02 01 00 99 98

Printed in the United States of America.

CONTENTS

IN HIS STEPS

*"*This is how we know we are in
him: Whoever claims to live in
him must walk as Jesus did."
—1 John 2:5b-6

In Charles Sheldon's classic novel *In His Steps,* the Reverend Henry Maxwell and a small group of Christians commit for an entire year to make all their choices based on this question: "What would Jesus do?"

The novel details the accounts of the characters' lives during an entire year after making that commitment. For some, the pledge brought misunderstanding, conflict, and suffering. For others, it inspired success in unexpected ways. But for all, it brought unprecedented joy and freedom.

In many ways, the goal of this book is to ask the same question as it applies to us as small-group leaders.

"What would Jesus do?"

You'll find that question laced through every activity, woven between the lines of every paragraph. As small-group leaders, it's a question we can't ignore. The answer in every situation we face provides the only true foundation for an "incarnational" ministry with youth.

At the end of his life, Jesus summed up the goal of his small-group ministry in a prayer to God. In his prayer, Jesus says, "I have revealed you to those whom you gave me out of the world. They were yours; you gave them to me and they have obeyed your word. Now they know that everything you have given me comes from you. For I gave them the words you gave me and they accepted them...As you sent me into the world, I have sent them into the world. For them I sanctify myself, that they too may be truly sanctified" (John 17:6-8a,18-19).

As "incarnational" small-group leaders, our goal is the same as Christ's:
- to help our kids understand and love God,
- to teach them to obey God's Word, and
- to send them into the world as God's followers.

Of course, we're all human. By our own strength, none of us is capable of following in Jesus' steps as a small-group leader. But we *can* be like Jesus if we humble ourselves and heed the words Jesus shared with the Apostle Paul: "My grace is sufficient for you, for my power is made perfect in weakness" (2 Corinthians 12:9b).

In the last few decades, small-group ministry has moved to the forefront of Christian culture. Small groups, usually of five to fifteen students from the same youth group, have become commonplace in youth ministry. In many ways, leading a small group has been honed to a science, complete with "essential elements" and "formulas" for success. These ideas have great merit and can provide genuine help for leaders who want to make their small groups successful. Sometimes, however, overdependence on formulas can cause us to lose sight of the truth that small groups are foundationally built on more personal connections—one-to-one relationships that cannot be effectively nurtured by simply combining the right mix of elements.

That's why the ideas in this book are specifically geared toward enhancing relationships among your small-group members. As a small-group leader, your freedom to help kids build deeper relationships is your greatest asset. While people who lead larger groups must sometimes rely on charisma and delegation to hold a group together, you have the opportunity to make disciples for God on a more intimate level. As Jesus did with his small group, you can also choose to open your life to *your* group members and pour into them all that God has poured into you.

Often it may mean taking kids on fun adventures (see "Rock Bonding" on page 104 and "Slice-of-Life Drama" on page 79) or simply spending "downtime" with them (see "Low-Key Getaway" on page 68).

But be warned. Following in Jesus' steps as a small-group leader can be risky. Some of the ideas you'll find in these pages will require courage and a level of vulnerability you may not have experienced before in your ministry. That's OK. You can grow right along with your kids as you try out these ideas. The payoff for you will be a closer, more meaningful relationship with God. And the payoff for your kids will be changed lives.

CHAPTER 1

LEARNING THROUGH EXPERIENCE

" Jesus knew that the Father had put all things under his power, and that he had come from God and was returning to God; so he got up from the meal, took off his outer clothing, and wrapped a towel around his waist. After that, he poured water into a basin and began to wash his disciples' feet, drying them with the towel that was wrapped around him. He came to Simon Peter, who said to him, 'Lord, are you going to wash my feet?' Jesus replied, 'You do not realize now what I am doing, but later you will understand.' "

—John 13:3-7

Experience is the gateway to wisdom. Or to bitterness. Or to hate or fear. The same storm that destroys two homes may cause one man to be more thankful for life, while his neighbor shakes her fist and curses God in anger. As one saying puts it, "The same rain that drowns the rat can grow the hay."

Ultimately, experience is a tool, not a teacher. We know this from the simple fact that not all old people are wise. Wisdom and learning come not from experience alone, but also from the correct interpretation and application of each experience to our lives.

Learning from experience is a matter of choice, not circumstance. That's why Jesus was able to make such a curious statement to Peter when the disciple balked at the thought of the Savior washing his feet: "You do not realize now what I am doing, but later you will understand."

Jesus knew Peter. He knew the wily fisherman would choose to learn all he could from this experience. It was as if Jesus were saying, "Don't be anxious about this, Peter. Just let yourself experience it for now. In time your heart will see what it all means, and you'll be changed."

The fact that Jesus used experience to teach his disciples is obvious from Scripture: walking on water (Matthew 14:22-33), cursing the fig tree (Matthew 21:18-22), chasing out the temple money-changers (Mark 11:15-18), and even feeding the five thousand (John 6:5-13). Christ's disciples shared in all of these experiences but fully understood them only in time.

Using experiences in this way to help someone grow can be called "seed teaching." Like seeds in the ground, the lessons from seed-teaching experiences are planted deep, then learned slowly, over time, like a seed that grows to maturity. But when the plant finally bears fruit—the lesson learned and applied—the result is a changed life.

Seed teaching is risky. Not everyone who goes through an experience will get the point. Some will simply forget about the experience—their seed is stolen. Some will interpret the experience incorrectly and fail to apply the lessons to their lives—their seed is choked. But some people who we guide through seed-teaching experiences will be changed. And they'll learn how to benefit from the experiences they'll encounter in the future.

Jesus knew the risks involved in teaching through experience, yet he chose to use it anyway. Why? Although his message of eternal life was for everyone, it was specifically aimed at those whose hearts were teachable and willing. He called it having "ears to hear." If some people's hearts were hardened against his message, he didn't try to sway them. Rather, the *way* he taught automatically sifted the crowds and drew out those whose hearts were willing. Teaching through experience is like that, too. Over time, it will change the hearts of those who are willing to be changed. And it will challenge the hearts of those who resist.

Consider your own walk with God. How many times has the Holy Spirit found a point of resistance in your heart and used experiences to expose it—again and again, if necessary? Each time we repent, we find ourselves saying, "How many times will I have to go through this before I learn?"

As the leader of a small group, seed teaching can work especially well. You have the ability to personalize experiences for your group members by talking with them about how each experience relates to their specific life situations. Having small groups also enables you to do a wider variety of experiences. For example, it wouldn't be feasible to take a large youth group to a woodworker's shop for personalized instruction from a craftsman. But, as you'll see later in the chapter, that experience can work wonderfully with a small group like yours.

Learning from experience is a powerful tool God still uses to influence willing hearts. You can use experiences to teach others, too, if you're willing. Remember, even with the advantages your small group has, not everyone may grasp the truth you're attempting to convey. But those who do will be changed forever.

Go ahead. Take the risk and be like Jesus.

GROUP-APPLICATION IDEAS

Use these real-life experiences to spur your group members toward deeper maturity in Christ. Pay close attention to the questions at the end of each experience. These will help you guide students to effectively interpret the experience and apply its lessons to their lives.

TIP BOX
Some of the ideas in this section may work in your locale and within your budget, while others may need adaptation to work in your setting. Use these ideas to spark your own creative alternatives!

FISHING TRIP

Help your teenagers learn what it means to be "fishers of men" by taking them on a fishing trip.

Talk to the congregation to find out which members are fishing fanatics. Ask these men and women to lend you their expertise by taking you and your group on a fishing trip. Try to have at least one trained fisherman (or woman) for every two or three students. Make sure you have enough equipment so everyone can participate (sharing is fine). You might ask students to provide a few dollars each to cover the cost of bait and lures (and fishing licenses if necessary—check the rules for your state).

Before the experience, ask the fishing experts to focus on teaching the group members basic fishing techniques and why different lures or baits work best at different times and with different fish. Encourage your experts to allow each person to fish long enough so that everyone has a good chance at catching a fish.

When you've finished fishing (and have something to show for it), have the experts teach the group members how to clean the fish and prepare them to eat. Make sure each person has a chance to get his or her hands dirty in the process.

After the experience, gather students together and ask:

● **What's your reaction to fishing? Explain.**
● **What surprised you most about this experience?**
● **What did you like least about this experience?**
● **What did you enjoy the most about this experience?**

Read aloud Luke 5:1-11. Ask:

• **What did Jesus mean when he told Peter he would start catching men instead of fish?** (Jesus was telling Peter about his mission; Jesus was letting Peter know that he was going to lead them on an adventure that affected people's lives.)

• **What lessons can you learn from fishing that can teach you about how God draws people to himself?** (God sets something good before people, just like the worm is set before the fish; we can fish all we want for people, but unless they go after the "food" on their own they won't be caught.)

• **What lessons can you learn from fishing that can teach you about how we as Christians should try to "catch" people for Christ?** (We need to be patient; we need to be persistent.)

• **What does fish-cleaning have to do with reaching people for Christ?** (Not everything about reaching people for Christ is pretty.)

• **How is cleaning a fish so it doesn't spoil like discipling new Christians? How is it different?** (If we don't disciple new Christians, they'll return to their old ways; it takes work to grow in Christ.)

• **How can learning about fishing change the way you relate to people as a Christian?**

• **What's one lesson from this experience you'll remember and apply to your life?**

TIP BOX

If you've had a banner fishing day, why not end the experience with a Southern fish fry? All you need is a nice outdoor spot, a pit fire, metal tongs, a large pot of hot cooking oil, corn meal, and eggs. Use the tongs to dip the fish in beaten eggs and then corn meal, then drop them in the oil until golden brown. Set out drinks, plates, forks, napkins, and, of course, tartar sauce. For entertainment, play horseshoes or volleyball.

If you decide not to have a fish fry, divide the fish among the group members for them to cook later on their own, or offer the fish to the fishing experts as thanks for their help.

HEART STAINS

Help teenagers learn how God feels about inward "dirtiness" through this unique experience.

TIP BOX

Some kids may initially seem resistant to the idea of putting mud on their faces. Strongly encourage them to participate. However, there may be one or two who won't join in no matter how much you coax them. That's OK. Allow them to travel with the group and participate just like all the others. Then use the optional debriefing questions at the end of the activity to help them process their choices.

Try this unusual experience on a Saturday when lots of people are out shopping. Have group members gather at someone's home. Explain to kids that they're going to go to the mall (or other shops around town) to run several minor errands. The trip isn't just for fun, however. It's part of an experiment in human nature.

Set out a large bowl of mud. Explain that you're going to decorate everyone's face with a small amount of mud before you leave. Kids must not remove the mud until all the day's events are finished.

Apply mud to each young person's face so that it's noticeable but not overwhelming. Then leave for the mall. Once you arrive, tell kids to look for ways the mud on their faces does (or doesn't) affect the way people treat them.

Lead kids through the mall for half an hour. Go through a major department store. At several points along the way, have a few group members leave the group to ask someone a question or to purchase a small item (such as a magazine or a snack). Tell kids to think about how they feel as they go off alone to interact with people in the mall (shoppers and store employees). Remember, even if a few group members don't wear the mud, have them go off alone and interact with strangers just as the other group members do.

Once everyone has had at least one solo interaction with a stranger, return to your church for debriefing. Don't allow kids to wipe off the mud yet. Ask:

● **What have you noticed about other people's reactions?**

● **What were you thinking as we all walked together through the mall?**

● **How is that different from the way you felt when you went off alone to interact with the people there?**

● **How did having mud on your face make you feel**

about yourself?

● Were you concerned about other people's reactions to you? Why or why not?

OPTIONAL QUESTIONS

If you had one or two young people who refused to wear the mud, ask them these questions:

● How did you feel walking around with us today?

● Did you ever wish you had mud on your face like the rest of us? Why or why not?

● What was your reaction to going off to talk to a stranger while we all watched?

● Were you concerned about what other people thought of you today? Why or why not?

Ask everyone:

● How is this mud on our faces similar to the things in our lives that we see as dirty or unsightly?

● What causes us to feel dirty about ourselves on the inside?

● How are your feelings today like the feelings you sometimes have when you let others get to know who you really are?

● How are your feelings today like the feelings you sometimes have when you pray?

Read aloud 1 Corinthians 6:9-11 and 1 Samuel 16:7. Then ask:

● What do these verses have to say about our inward dirtiness? (When we became Christians, we were cleansed; we constantly need to rid ourselves of "dirt.")

● How will God "wash" us if we let him? (God forgives our sin; God remakes us as "clean" people.)

● How would you be different if God washed away all the dirty places in your heart and life? (I'd be happier; I'd feel like a new person.)

Say: **Let's see what God's washing power might be like.**

Send all the group members to the restrooms and have them wash the mud off one another's faces. Make sure they don't wash the mud off themselves, even though having someone else do it may feel awkward.

Once everyone's face is clean, ask:

TIP BOX
To make the cleanup job easier, you may want to bring along a couple of hand towels for them to use—one for the girls and one for the guys.

- **Do you feel different? If so, how?**
- **How did it feel for someone else to clean the mud off your face?**
- **How would these feelings compare to allowing God to clean up our hearts?**
- **Even if God does wash our hearts, why is it still sometimes so hard for us to believe we're really clean?**
- **What's one thing you can do with God this week to move toward letting him in to clean up your heart?**

HOMELESS SEARCH

Help teenagers discover what it means to serve others.

This experience requires each group member to donate ten dollars.

TIP BOX

Many homeless people have a hard time getting around to different parts of town. Therefore, purchase your food certificates from a major grocery chain that has several stores all over town. This will make it easier for the homeless people to use them.

Have group members meet you at the church. Then go to a local supermarket and exchange the money for grocery certificates worth ten dollars. These certificates can be used to purchase food items, but they may not be used to buy either alcohol or tobacco. Give each person a ten-dollar certificate.

Once everyone has his or her certificate, lead kids on a search through your town for homeless or financially struggling people. Take kids to a homeless shelter if there is one in your town. Drive around the parts of town where homeless people are known to live. Once you find someone, send out two of your group members (and an adult sponsor) to give the person a ten-dollar certificate. Encourage kids to meet people they encounter and talk to them about how they became homeless. You'd be surprised how "normal" many homeless people are and how willing they are to talk about their situations.

Continue searching the area until kids have each had a chance to give away a certificate. If you have trouble locating enough homeless people, take kids to the homes of several elderly people in your church, and have them hand out their certificates.

Once all the certificates are given away, gather everyone together and ask:

● **What's your reaction to what we've done today?**

● **How is the way you feel now different from the way you felt when we started?**

● **Why do you think your feelings changed?**

● **What did you like most about today's experience?**

● **What was the most uncomfortable thing for you?**

● **Why is it often uncomfortable for us to show love to other people?**

Read aloud Matthew 10:40-42. Ask:

● **What is the reward Jesus is referring to in this passage?** (The reward of righteous living; the reward of everlasting life; the reward of God's blessing.)

● **What kind of reward have you received today for what you've done?** (God's blessing; a taste of what it means to live in God's kingdom.)

● **What greater reward is waiting in heaven for those who serve others the way we have today?** (Eternal life; a life without pain and suffering.)

● **What would have to change about your life or attitude for these kinds of experiences to become a regular part of your life?**

● **What can you pray for this week to start you on the road toward a lifestyle of giving to those less fortunate?**

TIP BOX

Many people are hesitant to give money or certificates to homeless people because they feel the homeless person may be operating a scam of some kind or may be involved in illegal activities. Although this is true only in some cases, it is possible that your young people may run into such a situation.

Rather than asking kids to discern whether a particular person is worth receiving the certificate, have them simply give the certificates to each of the people they approach. Have an adult sponsor go with them to present the gift.

As they approach each person, have kids say something like "I'm (name) from (name of your church). My small group is in your neighborhood today giving away these ten-dollar food certificates as a way of showing people God's love. Would you like one?"

HORSEBACK RIDING

Help teenagers explore how God can help them over-come bad situations.

Contact the equestrian centers in your area to find one that takes groups on guided horseback rides. (Even if you live in a large city, there's likely to be an equestrian center in your area.) Arrange a time to take your kids horseback riding.

At the end of the riding experience, gather kids together and ask:

TIP BOX

In case your group is unfamiliar with horses, or just for a fun time, get together to watch an older "cowboy" movie that includes lots of horseback-riding scenes.

- **How do you feel?**
- **What did you like most about this experience?**
- **What did you like the least?**
- **How does the power of the horse affect you?**
- **How would you feel if you rode a horse at full gallop?**
- **Why do you think ancient armies used horses so often?**

Read aloud Psalm 33:13-19. Then ask:

- **Why can't horses bring victory?** (Because God is the ultimate judge; might doesn't always win.)
- **In the Bible, a horse represented a method by which people added to their own strength in order to overcome obstacles. What are some "horses" people turn to today to make them feel more powerful?** (Money; prestige; drugs; control.)
- **What's your favorite "horse"?**
- **Why does the Bible say that depending on these things doesn't work?** (Because God is the only person we can depend on; these things are temporal.)
- **If depending on "horses" doesn't work for overcoming bad situations, what does?** (Trusting God; praying.)
- **What other parallels can you draw between the horses we rode today and the "horses" we turn to for strength in real life?**
- **How will you apply what you've learned to your life?**

NOBLE VESSELS

Help teenagers learn the importance of filling themselves with good thoughts and living out noble purposes.

For one of your small group meetings, have everyone bring a favorite mug or glass from home. If kids don't have a favorite, ask them simply to bring a nice glass or mug. At the meeting, have a chilled supply of kids' favorite drinks. Also bring a bowl of water, a bowl of dirt, and a clean glass of your own.

When everyone has arrived, take each glass or mug (except yours), dip it in the water, then coat it with the dirt. The dirtier the glasses become, the better. Set the glasses and mugs to the side to dry. Don't explain what you're doing. Use a strip of paper to mark each glass or mug so everyone knows who it belongs to.

While you're waiting for the glasses and mugs to dry, go around the room and take kids' drink orders. As kids place their orders, ask them why the drinks they chose are their favorites.

Once you have all the orders, fill the mugs and glasses with the selected beverages. Again, don't explain what you're doing, and ignore any questions kids have about the condition of the glasses and mugs.

Once you've distributed all the drinks, offer a brief prayer of thanks for the drinks, and read aloud Mark 14:23-25. Take a sip of your beverage. Then ask:

● **Do you want to drink your favorite drink from your favorite mug or glass? Why or why not?**

● **What's wrong with drinking from a dirty glass or mug?**

● **How did the verse I read affect your desire to drink?**

Read aloud 2 Timothy 2:20-22. Ask:

● **What are some wicked purposes that different containers in our lives have?** (Seeking selfish desires; pursuing only physical pleasure and ignoring spiritual matters.)

TIP BOX

One or two of your group members may drink from their dirty containers. That's OK (but don't let them take more than a sip). If they do drink, add these questions to the beginning of the discussion:

● Why did you drink from your glass even though it was dirty?

● What's your reaction to drinking from a dirty glass?

● How did you overcome your uneasiness about drinking from a dirty glass?

● **What are some noble purposes?** (Wanting to please God; reaching out to others in love.)

● **According to this passage, what makes a person's life noble or ignoble?** (The choices that person makes; who and what that person associates with.)

● **How is our experience with the glasses and mugs sometimes like God's experience with us when he wants to use us for noble purposes in real life?**

● **According to this passage, how can we cleanse ourselves so we can be used for noble purposes?**

Have kids go to the restrooms or kitchen to wash their containers. When they return, refill the containers with the appropriate drinks. Have kids enjoy their drinks as you ask:

● **Why is it so much easier to drink now?**

● **How is that like God's reaction when we cleanse our lives for his purposes?**

● **What are wicked things that distance you from God?**

● **What other parallels can you draw between our experience and the passages we've read?**

● **What can you do this week to apply what you've learned to your life?**

SAILING

Help teenagers discover how the Holy Spirit can guide them in life.

Take kids sailing on a lake in your area. If you live in a large city, you can make this experience part of a weekend retreat to the country. If possible use smaller sailboats (these can be rented by the hour or the day) so each young person can actively participate in the sailing experience. Have kids take turns working the sail and the rudder.

After a full day of sailing fun, gather kids around a campfire for a hot dog roast and discussion. Ask:

● **What's your reaction to sailing?**

● **What makes it exciting and unpredictable?**

● **How is sailing like a picture of the life of a Christian?**

Read aloud John 3:8. Ask:

- **If the wind is like the Spirit of God, what might our sail represent? our rudder?** (Our willingness to follow God; our desire to learn more about following God; the Bible.)
- **Is it possible for a sailboat to be "dead in the water" even when the wind is blowing? Explain.** (Yes, if the sail isn't up; yes, if the person doesn't know which direction to face.)
- **How is that like how we are sometimes?**
- **In sailing, can you always choose your direction? Why or why not?**
- **How is that like following God's Spirit in life?**
- **What other parallels can you draw from sailing that can apply to your walk with God?**
- **How can you use this experience to grow in your faith this month?**

SENDING OUT

Help teenagers develop their Christlike abilities to meet others' needs.

Arrange for an adult driver and transportation for every two people in your group. Form pairs and connect each pair with a driver.

Then give kids these simple instructions: **With your driver, go find someone who has a genuine need and meet it.**

Tell pairs they have one hour to complete their tasks. Then have them report back to the church. (Tasks might include raking leaves, shopping for a shut-in, cleaning a garage, or preparing a meal.)

When all the pairs have reported in, have them relate their experiences to the rest of the group.

After everyone has shared, ask:
- **What did you learn about yourself through this experience?**

- **What did you learn about the people you encountered?**
- **Would you do this experience again? Why or why not?**

Have volunteers take turns reading aloud Matthew 10:1-16. Ask:

- **How was our experience like the disciples' experience in this passage? How was it different?** (We were sent out to meet others' needs; the disciples didn't have the benefit of knowing Christ's reason for their mission.)
- **What does it mean for Christians today to have authority in Christ?** (We can live our faith confidently; the Holy Spirit empowers us to reach out with God's love.)
- **What kind of authority did you experience today?**
- **How is that like the disciples' authority in this passage? How is that different?**

Read aloud Matthew 10:32-42. Ask:

- **What does this passage say about the experience we just had?**
- **How is serving others an expression of authority in Christ?**
- **What other parallels can you draw between your experience and the disciples' experience?**
- **Will your life be changed because of what you've learned today? Why or why not?**

WALK-ON-WATER LAKE RACE

Help teenagers learn what it means to trust God. Choose a small pond or placid river, one to two feet deep, for this fun experience. Plan for the event by explaining to kids that you're going to sponsor a walk-on-water race across a pond. Have kids form teams of two or three for the event.

The rules are simple: Team members must walk together across the pond, using any homemade methods they can create. For example, kids might try making inflated inner tube shoes, or they might create floating water skis by strapping boards to air mattresses. The items they use must be homemade and must allow them to actually walk on the water with no outside support.

The day of the race have teams prepare on one side of the pond or river. On the opposite side of the pond, place a flag or some other item for kids to aim for. (Important: require all participants to wear life jackets.)

The first team to cross the water and grab the flag wins the race. Teams that fall in the water must start over.

Chances are, few in your group will be able to do this successfully, but it will be fun to try!

After the race, congratulate all the teams on their ingenuity and effort. Then gather everyone together and ask:

● **How did it feel to stand on the water?**

● **Did you trust your water-walking invention? Why or why not?**

● **What did you learn about yourself in this experience? about your teammates?**

Read aloud Matthew 14:22-33. Then ask:

● **How was Peter's experience like ours today?** (We lose faith easily; God calls us to trust.)

● **How was it different?** (Our lives have less drama; we face different situations.)

● **Which experience would you rather have—ours or Peter's? Explain.**

● **What are ways we try to walk on water today without looking to God for strength?**

● **Why don't we depend on God for strength to do impossible things?**

● **What caused Peter to start sinking?**

● **What causes us to start sinking in our own lives?**

● **What lessons can you learn from your experience today that can help your relationship with God?**

● **What other comparisons can you draw between our experience today and Peter's experience in the Bible?**

● **What spiritual principles have we discovered today that can make a difference in our lives this week?**

WOODWORKER'S SHOP

Help teenagers explore how God shapes them. If you aren't familiar with anyone in your church who has a woodworking hobby, check out the Yellow Pages under "Woodworking" for artisans in your area. Once you've established contact, ask the woodworker if you can bring members of your small group to the workshop for a hands-on demonstration. Most woodworkers will be excited to share knowledge of their craft with your kids—probably in hopes that one of them will take up the craft as well.

Once you've discussed equipment and safety issues with the woodworker, ask him or her if kids can each bring a small block of wood to be shaped. For example, with proper supervision, kids can use a band saw to turn a simple section of one-by-six-inch wood into a dinosaur-shaped pencil holder. Or the woodworker can use a small lathe to turn a small block of wood into a wooden vase.

TIP BOX

Although the woodworker can focus on only one young person at a time, you can keep everyone working by having kids use sandpaper to smooth out their creations, then apply paint, stain, or finish to the wood. Also, encourage kids to watch as their companions' creations are being made.

Set up a time for the outing, and have interested kids sign liability-release forms (p. 23). Also ask each person to bring a solid section of wood suitable for woodworking.

Once at the woodworker's shop, have the artisan teach kids about his or her craft. Then, under the woodworker's guidance, have each person create something from his or her block of wood.

When young people have finished their creations, have them help the woodworker clean the workshop and then thank the woodworker for offering his or her expertise. Once you've returned to the church, have students gather and explain their creations by telling what they started with, how they shaped them, and what they are planning to use them for. Then ask:

● **What surprised you about this experience?**

● **What did you like most about woodworking?**

● **We all know that Jesus was skilled in woodworking. What do you think he enjoyed about it?**

● **How is the way we shaped our wood like the way God shapes us?**

LIABILITY RELEASE FORM

Release of All Claims

In consideration for being accepted by _____ for participation in

(Church name)

_____, we (I), being 21 years of age or older, do for ourselves

(Name of trip or activity)

(myself) (and for and on behalf of my child-participant if said child is not 21 years of age or older)

do hereby release, forever discharge and agree to hold harmless _____

(Church name)

and the directors thereof from any and all liability, claims or demands for personal injury, sickness or death, as well as property damage and expenses, of any nature whatsoever which may be incurred by the undersigned and the child-participant that occur while said child is participating in the above-described trip or activity.

Furthermore, we (I) (and on behalf of our (my) child-participant If under the age of 21 years] hereby assume all risk of personal injury, sickness, death, damage and expense as a result of participation in recreation and work activities involved therein.

Further, authorization and permission is hereby given to said church to furnish any necessary transportation, food and lodging for this participant.

The undersigned further hereby agree to hold harmless and indemnify said church, its directors, employees and agents, for any liability sustained by said church as the result of the negligent, willful or intentional acts of said participant, including expenses incurred attendant thereto.

(If the participant has not attained the age of 21 years):

We (I) are the parent(s) or legal guardian(s) of this participant, and hereby grant our (my) permission for him (her) to participate fully in said trip, and hereby give our (my) permission to take said participant to a doctor or hospital and hereby authorize medical treatment, including but not in limitation to emergency surgery or medical treatment, and assume the responsibility of all medical bills, if any.

Further, should it be necessary for the participant to return home due to medical reasons, disciplinary action or otherwise, we (I) hereby assume all transportation costs.

_____

(Type or print name of participant)

_____

[Parent(s) telephone]

(Only participant need sign if 21 years of age or older. If under 21, *both* parents must sign unless parents are separated or divorced in which case the custodial parent must sign.)

_____

(Pastor's telephone)

_____

Father   Date

Hospital insurance ❑ Yes ❑ No

Insurance company

_____

Mother   Date

Policy number _____

Physician _____

Physician's phone _____

Emergency phone numbers _____

_____

Legal guardian   Date

_____

Participant, if age 21   Date

Trip Participant Only

I have read the foregoing and understand the rules of conduct for participants and will abide by them as well as the directions of the leadership of the trip.

_____

Participant

- If we are like the wood when God shapes us, what might we compare the wood shavings to in our own lives?
- After our wood was shaped, we still had to sand it down to prevent splinters. How is that also like God's shaping process in our lives?
- What happened when you encountered a knot in the wood?
- How is that like what happens when God encounters resistance in our lives?
- What can this experience teach us about ways God shapes our lives?
- How will this experience change the way you live?

YOUTH GARDEN

Help teenagers discover what it takes to grow in Christ.

Ask the church leaders for a small area of ground to use as a youth garden. Be sure to explain to the leaders why you want to use the space and how you expect the group members to benefit. Advertise the garden to your group. Explain that you want to distribute the produce grown in the garden to the poor in your community or to the neighbors around your church.

In early spring, divide the plot of land into four equal sections. To one section, do nothing. Have students till and weed the other three sections and prepare them for planting.

Allow kids to decide what plants they'd like to grow, but encourage them to choose produce that can be immediately consumed with little or no preparation. For example, carrots, peanuts, melons, or strawberries would all work better than squash, potatoes, or cabbage.

When the time comes for planting, have kids follow these guidelines for each section:
- Section 1 (the untilled section)—Scatter seeds on the ground. Don't push them into the soil.
- Section 2—Plant the seeds no deeper than one-quarter inch below the surface.

• Section 3—Plant the seeds according to the directions on the seed package but also plant weeds among the seeds. (You probably won't be able to find weeds in seed form, so just transplant several weeds from another location.)

• Section 4—Plant the seeds according to the directions on the seed package. Make sure this section is free of weeds.

After the initial planting and watering, have kids follow these instructions in tending each section:

• Section 1—Do nothing.
• Section 2—Do nothing.
• Section 3—Water as often as needed, and allow the weeds to grow freely.
• Section 4—Water as often as needed, and keep the ground free of weeds and insects.

When harvest time comes, have a first-fruits party for the farmers. After gathering all the produce, allow each farmer to sample the produce. Then divide the produce into gift sacks and deliver the items as gifts to the church's neighbors or to a homeless shelter in your community.

After delivering the gift sacks, return to the garden. As students inspect each section, ask:

• **What stands out to you as you look at our garden?**
• **What did you like about gardening?**
• **What did you dislike about it?**

Read aloud Matthew 13:3-9. Ask:

• **How are our four sections like the four soils described in this passage?** (Some plants died; only the cared-for plants survived.)

• **What does this experience have to do with growing in Christ?** (We need to work at growing; we need to learn more about Christ to grow.)

• **What do the seeds represent in our lives?**

• **What does the soil represent?**

• **How does the condition of the**

TIP BOX

In order to time the harvest correctly, be sure to choose fruits or vegetables that grow and mature at roughly the same rate. That way you'll avoid having some produce spoil while you're waiting for other items to mature.

TIP BOX

Rather than creating a rotating schedule in which "farmers" trade off weeks in caring for the garden, encourage each participant to spend time in the garden each week. Keeping students involved through the whole process will help them get the most out of the experience. Perhaps set up "garden-care" times each week (such as on worship-day mornings and midweek Bible study nights). During these times have kids work together to tend the garden.

soil, and the way we tend it, affect how well the seed can grow?

- How is that like the way we grow spiritually?
- Which section was easiest to care for?
- Which section provided the most produce?
- How might that apply to anything in real life?
- How do we make ourselves like the soil in section 1? section 2? section 3? section 4?
- What have you learned about yourself from this experience?
- How will this experience change the way you live?

CHAPTER 2

ASKING
THE RIGHT
QUESTIONS

"When Jesus came to the region of Caesarea Philippi, he asked his disciples, 'Who do people say the Son of Man is?' They replied, 'Some say John the Baptist; others say Elijah; and still others, Jeremiah or one of the prophets.' 'But what about you?' he asked. 'Who do you say I am?' Simon Peter answered, 'You are the Christ, the Son of the living God.' "

—Matthew 16:13-16

What's in a question?

Mystery. Challenge. Exposure. Curiosity. And, if you're teachable, growth.

The most obvious reason we ask questions is, of course, to find answers. But it isn't the only reason, nor is it always the most important. If it were, we would never ask questions such as "What lies beyond infinity?" or "Why did God take my daughter away?" Questions like that probably have no answers this side of eternity—yet we ask them anyway.

Sometimes it's the unanswerable questions that impact us the most. And sometimes it's the difficult questions that force our hearts to change—whether we want them to or not. The truth is that questions can do far more in our lives than simply reveal information. For example:

● They can open doorways in the heart to new possibilities: "Do you believe that I am able to do this?" (Matthew 9:28).

● They can cause the soul to look at itself and the world around it in new ways: "Woman, where are they? Has no one condemned you?" (John 8:10).

● They can challenge set ways of thinking and expose broken places in people's hearts: "And why do you break the command of God for the sake of your tradition?" (Matthew 15:3).

● And, most importantly, they can cause us to grapple with mysteries that cannot be fully understood this side of eternity: " 'You of little faith,' he said, 'why did you doubt?' " (Matthew 14:31).

Jesus used questions all the time—as a tool to teach people, to encourage them, to challenge them, and to expose their sins. Consider this quote by J. Dennis Miller, taken from the book *Discipling the Young Person:*

> Jesus asked questions *ten times* more than he gave answers. This was the Son of God, who had at least ten times more *answers* than questions! Isn't that ironic? God, in the flesh, comes to earth and lives among us, knowing the solutions, knowing the answers—yet He asks questions![1]

Jesus did indeed have the answers. But he knew that those answers would seem meaningless unless his followers first understood the questions. As Christ's disciples, we know that the answer the world needs is Jesus. But what kind of meaning is that answer going to have for the young man who's asking, "How can I look 'cool' to my friends?" or the young woman who's asking, "How can I make myself beautiful so guys will be attracted to me?"

First we have to ask the right questions. Only then will the answers make sense.

Jesus understood this principle. Consequently, when someone asked him a question, he often responded with another question to challenge wrong thinking or help guide the questioner toward deeper understanding.

So what does all this have to do with you and your small group? Everything. Like Jesus, you can use questions as a tool in your small group to propel kids' hearts toward God. Asking good questions can be one of the easiest skills you develop as a small-group leader, and yet it is also one of the most powerful.

In his ministry on earth, Jesus generally used questions to do one of four things:

● to teach (Matthew 22:41-46),

● to challenge wrong thinking (Matthew 5:46-48),

● to expose the darkness in people's hearts (Luke 20:2-8), and

● to encourage faith (John 5:2-6).

Take a few minutes now to read through each of those passages. Get a feel for why and how Jesus used questions in each situation. Notice that sometimes he never really expected an answer!

As a small-group leader, you have a special advantage when it comes to asking questions. Because of your group's size, you can use questions to focus in on each person's needs, asking specific questions for specific hearts, just like Jesus did.

But what if you're not that creative, you ask? What if you aren't able to cause deep, thought-provoking questions to appear magically in your head on a moment's notice? What should you do then?

Don't worry. It isn't as hard as you think. Try the application ideas provided in this chapter. And remember, you have the Spirit of Christ within you to give you help whenever you need it.

GROUP-APPLICATION IDEAS

Use these ideas to make "Jesus-style" questions a significant part of your small-group ministry.

LIFE'S LITTLE MYSTERIES

Set up a bulletin board in your meeting room, and title it "Life's Little Mysteries." Over the next several weeks, challenge kids to come up with questions that can't be answered and submit them to you for consideration. If you think any question is genuinely "unanswerable," post it on the board for all to ponder.

For example, kids might submit questions such as "Why does God allow babies to be born with severe disabilities?" or "Why does iced tea cost as much as a soft drink in a restaurant?" For each question you accept, award kids with a coupon for their favorite coffee house or ice-cream shop.

Take time to discuss the unanswerable questions with your group from time to time. Ask the teenagers why the questions are unanswerable and what they can learn from the "unanswerability" of the questions.

PASS THE SACK

At a small-group gathering, use this activity in place of your regular activities to help kids learn more about each other and how to ask questions.

Photocopy the list of questions on page 31, then cut them apart. Place the question strips in a paper sack so kids can draw out questions one at a time.

At the meeting have kids form a circle. Then pass the sack around the room. As each person gets the sack, have him or her draw out a question, read it aloud, and answer it. Then have kids place the questions back in the sack. Continue until everyone has answered at least three questions or until time is up.

QUESTIONS

- What's one of your most memorable childhood experiences?

- If you could change one thing about your past, what would it be?

- If you could control one thing about your future on earth, what would it be?

- What's one fact about yourself that nobody knows?

- What one positive word best describes your father?

- What one positive word best describes your mother?

- How are you different from the rest of your family?

- If you could change anything about your family, what would you change?

- What's one dream you want to come true before you die?

- If you could change one quality about yourself, what would you change?

- What's the most important thing in your life? Explain.

- What makes you a good choice for friendship?

- What's one goal you have for yourself this year?

- What's one thing you wish were different in your life right now?

- What do you want people to say about you after you're dead?

QUESTIONS BY JESUS

Study the questions Jesus asked during his ministry on earth. Ask teenagers to imagine themselves in Jesus' place as he faced each situation so they can better understand why Jesus chose to ask the questions he did instead of simply giving answers.

Encourage teenagers to use the following references as the basis for a daily devotion time. Have group members keep journals of their reactions to Jesus' questions and insights into Jesus' reasons for asking the questions.

Here are several passages that contain Jesus' questions:

Matthew 5:46-47
Matthew 6:25-30
Matthew 7:3-4
Matthew 8:23-26
Matthew 9:1-7
Matthew 9:27-30
Matthew 15:1-9
Matthew 16:13-20
Matthew 16:26
Matthew 20:20-23
Matthew 22:41-46
Matthew 26:50-54
Mark 3:1-6
Mark 3:31-35
Mark 4:35-40
Mark 8:11-13
Mark 8:14-21
Mark 10:46-52

Mark 12:13-17
Luke 6:46-49
Luke 11:11-13
Luke 12:25-26
Luke 12:54-57
Luke 13:10-16
Luke 18:7-8
Luke 22:48
John 6:1-6
John 7:19
John 7:21-24
John 8:1-11
John 8:45-47
John 9:35-38
John 10:31-32
John 13:37-38
John 21:15-23

PERSON-IN-THE-MALL INTERVIEWS

Using either an audiocassette recorder or a video camera, send group members out into the local mall or shopping center to interview shoppers by asking them the same questions Jesus asked.

Refer to the "Questions by Jesus" activity on page 32 for a list of passages that contain Jesus' questions. From this list choose five or six questions for teenagers to ask passers-by. Modernize Jesus' questions where necessary to make them easier for people to understand. For example, "What good is it for a man to gain the whole world, yet forfeit his soul?" (Mark 8:36) might be changed to "What good can come to a person who gains fame, wealth, or power, but at the cost of his or her soul?"

After the interviews, gather group members together to review people's responses. After kids have listened to what people said, ask:

- **What's your reaction to these people's responses?**
- **Do you think their responses were sincere? Why or why not?**
- **Which responses surprised you?**
- **What do these responses say about the way most people look at life?**
- **Were these people's responses to these questions the same as yours might be? Why or why not?**
- **As Christians, what's different about our perspective on life?**
- **If you could tell the people we interviewed anything you wanted, what would you tell them?**
- **How might this experience help us share our faith with others more effectively?**
- **How can using questions like these help us in sharing our faith with others?**

QUESTION CURRICULUM

At a regular group meeting, ask kids to provide you with questions they'd like to have answered about God, life, relationships, or the world. Encourage kids to submit as many questions as they can think of.

Once you've collected a hefty list, organize the questions by categories, and rank them according to how many times they were asked. Then use the questions as the basis for organizing your curriculum in the coming months.

One way you could do this is to find separate youth studies that address each of the questions kids have asked and organize them into a comprehensive curriculum. Or you could choose one thorough curriculum system and supplement it with your own material addressing kids' questions.

As a reference for your group, write on newsprint all the questions kids have asked, and post the newsprint on the wall of the meeting room. Then, as each question is answered to kids' satisfaction, use a marker to check it off. Remind kids that sometimes questions can't be answered fully until God "fills in the blanks" in the new kingdom.

 # QUESTION EXCHANGE

At one of your group meetings, pass out pencils and stacks of index cards to kids. On their cards have kids write out anonymous questions for specific people in the group to answer. A question can be about anything connected to that person's life or faith in God. Don't have kids sign their names on the cards. Instead, have them write on each card the name of the person to whom the question is addressed.

Once kids have turned in their cards, flip through them and screen out any questions that might be offensive or embarrassing. Then read aloud the questions, addressing each one to the appropriate person for him or her to answer. Allow group members to ask as many follow-up questions as they like. Continue until all the questions have been answered.

QUESTION OF THE WEEK

At the start of each group meeting, write a "question of the week" for kids to grapple with. Have kids form groups of two or three to discuss the question and come up with responses. Make sure kids understand that not everyone in their group has to agree on one response to the question, but everyone should share an opinion.

Here are a few examples of questions you might use. Feel free to use these or any others you find in the Scriptures that might apply.

• **"If Jesus were in the flesh today—living incognito— do you think he'd be welcomed into our church? Why or why not?"**

• **"How are you most like Jesus? What needs to change so that you can become more like him?"**

• **"If you believe God is your protector and provider, why do you fear?"**

• **"Why do most people get more excited at a ballgame than they do at church?"**

• **"How can people tell you're a Christian?"**

RELIVING THE STORY

Join kids in watching a movie such as *The Greatest Story Ever Told* or *Jesus,* or something similar. Stop the movie frequently as you're watching, and ask kids questions such as these:

• **How would you be reacting right now in this situation?**

• **What would you do if you were Jesus?**

• **What would you say to Jesus right now, if you could say anything?**

TIP BOX

It's a good idea to preview any movie on the life of Christ before you choose to show it to your kids. Check the movie for biblical accuracy, and make a note of any scenes in the film that don't line up with what really happened. Then, when you watch the movie, stop the film at those scenes and explain to kids what really occurred. Then ask:

• **Why do you think the movie makers changed the facts in this scene?** →

- How does knowing what really happened affect the way you see Jesus? your own faith?

- **What surprises you about Jesus in this scene?**

SITE QUESTIONS

Take kids on special field trips to help them confront tough questions about their faith. For example, have kids visit a state mental hospital or a terminal ward at the regular hospital. Then ask:

- **Why does God allow mental illness?**
- **Why does God allow deformities?**
- **Why does God allow suffering?**
- **How should Christians respond to these things?**

Or have kids visit an orphanage for a day. Encourage kids to play with the children and pray for them individually. Then ask:

- **How does God reach out to abandoned or orphaned children?**
- **Why don't these children have families?**
- **Why would God allow this?**

Or take kids on a tour of a prison. Ask the prison chaplain to join you and explain to your group the types of backgrounds most inmates come from. Then ask:

- **Why are some people given an easier upbringing than others?**
- **What determines the worth of a person?**
- **Based on what you've seen here, what should you be doing with your own life?**

YOUR-WORLD QUESTIONNAIRE

Ask all the members of your group to fill out a "Your-World Questionnaire" (p. 38). Use the information from these questionnaires to better understand how your kids see the world and how they perceive themselves in it. After you've learned a bit about your young people, set up meetings with each person in your group. At the meetings ask kids to expound on what they wrote in their questionnaires. Also ask additional questions that accomplish one of the four purposes for which Jesus used questions (see p. 38).

Use your meetings as a foundation for an ongoing discussion with kids about their lives. Rather than hand out "right" answers to kids with faulty beliefs, use questions to challenge kids to seek out answers on their own.

(see p. 38)

TIP BOX

As you read through kids' questionnaires, you may come across some serious belief problems in kids' lives. Rather than confronting them with the "right" belief, ask challenging questions such as these:

● **What led you to believe this idea was true?**
● **Do you know what the Bible teaches on this issue?**
● **How do you reconcile what you believe with what the Bible teaches?**

Help guide kids through this process by meeting with them individually every six weeks. At those meetings, ask follow-up questions about kids' lives and continue to challenge them to seek out God's truth.

Endnote
[1] J. Dennis Miller, *Discipling the Young Person,* ed. Paul Fleischmann (San Bernardino, CA: Here's Life Publishers, Inc., 1985), 64.

Your-World Questionnaire

Name:

Address:

Phone:

Birthday:

Age:

1. What do you think is the most important issue facing the world today?

2. What's the biggest issue you are facing in your life right now?

3. How do you live out your Christianity from day to day?

4. Do you think Christianity is better than other types of beliefs? Why or why not?

5. What do you think makes someone a Christian?

6. What do you believe about sex before marriage?

7. What do you believe about homosexuality?

8. What do you believe about abortion?

9. What's one positive thing you'd like to see happen in the world this year?

10. What's one positive thing you'd like to see happen in your life this year?

11. Do you know your purpose in life? If so, what is it? If not, why not?

12. What's one question about life you wish you understood better?

PACKAGING TRUTH IN PARABLES

"The disciples came to him and asked, 'Why do you speak to the people in parables?' He replied, 'The knowledge of the secrets of the kingdom of heaven has been given to you, but not to them. Whoever has will be given more, and he will have an abundance. Whoever does not have, even what he has will be taken from him. This is why I speak to them in parables: Though seeing, they do not see; though hearing, they do not hear or understand.' "

—Matthew 13:10-13

Jesus' use of parables, although masterful, can also seem confusing to Christians today. And we're not the first to feel that way. Even the original twelve disciples were often baffled by Jesus' parables. They asked him about them, but his answer seemed only to add to their questions. Was Jesus really using parables to *hide* the truth from people? Why would he want to do that? Didn't he come to reveal the truth—not cover it up?

Before we can answer the question of why, we first have to be sure of what a parable is. For instance, is it an analogy? a simple word picture? Although a parable has elements of each of these, it is neither of them exactly.

- A parable is, in essence, *a truth wrapped in a story*. That's different from a word picture, which generally focuses on describing scenes or feelings rather than truths. It also differs from an analogy, which is usually aimed at comparing a situation or feeling with another rather than illustrating a truth.

- Parables describe eternal truths in common ways so that teachable hearts can understand and embrace those truths. And also—as Jesus points out in Matthew 13:10-13—so proud hearts will reject those truths.

That's why Jesus gave such a peculiar response to the disciples' question. "Whoever has," Jesus said, "will be given more, and he will have an abundance. Whoever does not have, even what he has will be taken from him."

What did Jesus mean by this? Whoever has *what* will be given more? Whoever doesn't have *what* will lose even what he has?

- Consider the context of Jesus' words. He had just finished explaining to his disciples the parable of the sower. He had just finished telling them how some people have "good soil" and others have "bad soil." The "seed" of the Word is stolen away or choked out by bad soil, but that same seed takes root in good soil and produces an abundant crop.

- Understanding this, Jesus' next words now make more sense. Why does he teach in parables? So that "whoever has [good soil] will be given more, and he will have an abundance." And "whoever does not have [good soil], even what he has will be taken from him."

- Parables are simply seeds of truth presented in their most basic form. Parables illustrate truths in such a simple way that it's difficult *not* to understand them (provided you don't try to make them more complicated than they are). Even so, only those with good soil—that is, humble, teachable hearts—can receive truth and be changed by it. When the truth contained in a parable falls on bad soil—a proud, self-righteous heart—it's quickly stolen away by pride or choked to death by worldly concerns.

So why should you use parables in your small group? For the same reasons Jesus did—because parables illustrate truth in simple, understandable ways and because they expose the pride in people's hearts. While many people may understand a parable, only someone who's humble will embrace the truth contained within it and be changed.

Parables can be particularly effective in a small-group setting because of the individual contact you have with kids. You can shape your parables around things your kids are most familiar with. For example, if some of your group members work with horses, you can create a parable about horses that relates to kids' lives (see Psalm 32:8-9). Or if some of your group members are on the track team, you can create a parable about running that illustrates a truth in the Bible (see Jeremiah 12:5 and 1 Corinthians 9:24-25).

God still uses parables today to teach his followers. God's creation is filled with parables—each one illustrating a truth for us to understand and embrace. By opening your hearts to become childlike and teachable, you can uncover the eternal truths that are being illustrated all around you every day. And you can use the same parables that have helped you to help your kids as well.

GROUP-APPLICATION IDEAS

Use these sample parables to enrich your ministry with kids and inspire you to create teaching parables of your own.

BEACHCOMBER PARABLE

The kingdom of God is like a man who went for a walk through the shallow waters of the beach. As he walked, the force of the waves rocked his body, and he quickly looked down at the surf around his feet to try to regain his balance. But the churning water confused his eyes, so he fell. He stood up and once more tried to walk through the surf. This time, when the waves rocked his body, he kept his eyes focused straight ahead upon the horizon. As long as he did this, his steps did not falter.

Anyone who's been on a beach knows this experience. Looking down as you walk through the surf causes you to feel disoriented. Your brain is tricked into thinking you're losing your balance, so you do. You have to keep your eyes focused on where you're headed to keep from falling over.

That's just how it is in our Christian lives, too. Whenever we take our eyes off Jesus and focus on the turbulent events happening around us, we're bound to stumble. But by keeping our hearts focused on him alone, we stay true to his course for our lives.

For the biblical basis for this parable, read Hebrews 12:1-3 and Matthew 14:22-33.

EAGLE PARABLE

TIP BOX

As soon as you're able, begin developing your own collection of parables. As your collection grows, record them in a card file organized by topic and Bible basis. Here are a few tips to help you get started:

● Study Jesus' parables, then modernize them to use with today's kids.

● Search the Old Testament for parables. For example, many great parables are found in the prophetic books, such as Isaiah and Jeremiah.➜

The kingdom of God is like a mother eagle that builds her nest high up on the mountainside. When her hatchling grows strong enough, she pushes it over the edge of the nest so it plummets toward the ground. If the hatchling does not spread its wings and catch the air, the mother eagle swoops down beneath it and carries it on her back all the way up to the nest.

As soon as the hatchling is safely back in the nest, the mother eagle again pushes it off the edge and lets it fall, catching it once again if it does not fly. She continues to do this until the young bird learns how to spread its wings, catch the wind, and soar just as she does.

This real-life example from nature provides a wonderful picture of how faith develops in our lives. In the same way that the young bird learns to depend on the air, which it cannot see, we also learn to depend on something we can't see (God) and spread our "wings" of faith.

For the biblical basis for this parable, read Isaiah 40:31 and Hebrews 11:1.

● Ask God to help you see parables in the world around you. Take time to watch children at play, observe a thunderstorm, or watch the effects of fire or wind on the world around you. Ask God, "How is this like you or some aspect of Christian faith?"

FOOD PARABLE

The kingdom of God is like a nameless man who lived on the streets, eating insects and rancid garbage. One day his father, who had been searching for him for years, found him in a back alley, took him home, and gave him healthy food to eat. At first the healthy food was unbearable to the nameless man because he was used to living on garbage. But the more he ate the healthy food, the more he desired it, and the healthier he became. Eventually he came to crave healthy food, and he despised the garbage he used to eat.

This natural parable illustrates what happens to people who are rescued from habitual sin and turn to follow God. At first, obeying God seems impossible, and the pull of the old life seems overwhelming. But with patience, old things lose their flavor, and the sweetness of following Christ becomes our driving motivation.

For a biblical basis for this parable, read Proverbs 4:18; Romans 12:1-2; and 2 Corinthians 3:17-18.

LEPROSY PARABLE

Life without God is like a woman with leprosy, who slowly destroyed her own body because she was no longer sensitive to touch or to pain.

This short parable provides a graphic illustration of what happens to people's hearts when they try to survive without God and get caught up in sin. The woman's body represents her life; the leprosy represents her calloused heart. A heart that's not sensitive to God becomes numb to life and eventually destroys itself, no matter how hard it tries to survive.

For a biblical basis for this parable, read Romans 6:15-23 and 8:5-14.

MAN-IN-THE-MIRROR PARABLE

A person coming face to face with sin in his or her life is like a man walking toward a mirror. The closer he gets, the more clearly he can see his true reflection.

Coming to terms with the darkness in our hearts is the first step toward receiving God's healing and restoration. Only when kids really look at the sin in their lives can they begin to know who they really are outside of God.

Conversely, once a person has received Christ and is walking with him, the parable changes. Then, discovering our true identity comes by looking at Jesus—not at our sin.

For a biblical basis for this parable, read 2 Corinthians 3:17-18 and James 1:23-25.

MOUNTAIN PARABLE

The Christian life is like a man who inherited a vast, beautiful, mountainous land. The mountains of the land were too large and wonderful to see from the ground, so the man located the highest peak in the land and prepared to climb it. Knowing the climb would be long and difficult, he sold all he owned and bought the best supplies for his journey.

When he was ready, he started his climb. The way was steep, and trees and rocks obstructed any view of the vast land the man had inherited. Most of the time, he stared at the patch of ground directly in front of him.

Before long the man became exhausted and collapsed. He quickly realized that if he was ever going to make it to the top, he'd have to leave his expensive provisions behind. So he took off his pack and left all his supplies sitting in the dirt.

The way became easier. The longer the man climbed, the stronger he became and the more he began to enjoy climbing. Occasionally he would catch a glimpse of his beautiful land, and he would weep for joy before continuing up the mountain.

Finally, after a long and patient journey, he reached the top and looked out over the endless mountains that stretched out before him. The beauty of the land overwhelmed him. And at that moment, he committed his life to climbing all the peaks in the whole land, one at a time, until he had known them all.

This parable illustrates how the Christian life is a constant adventure, full of risk and the possibility of failure, but also full of unparalleled beauty and splendor. The mountains represent our "inheritance" in Christ, and the many daring challenges that come with it. The climber represents us. The more deeply the climber explores the land, the more the land changes him, until it becomes the passion of his life.

For the biblical basis for this parable, read 2 Corinthians 3:7-18 and Hebrews 12:1-29.

NUMB-HEARTS PARABLE

The effect of sin on a person's heart is like the woman who fell in love with a beautiful jewel. The jewel was secured on a golden stand in the middle of a grand auditorium, with one powerful light shining down on all its brilliance. The jewel was so revered by all the people that anyone who entered the room had to remove his or her shoes and gaze at it from a distance.

Since the jewel could not be moved from its place, the woman decided to move closer and marvel at the jewel there on its stand.

As the woman approached the jewel, she did not realize the floor was embedded with razor-sharp shards of glass that protruded from the floor. She was so enraptured by the jewel's beauty that at first she didn't even notice the deep cuts on her feet from the shards. Then, suddenly screaming in pain, the woman fled from the jewel and fell to the ground because of the pain in her feet.

At first she didn't want to get up ever again, but soon the beauty of the jewel enticed her to rise. And once again she crossed the shard-filled floor to gaze at the jewel. And again the shards cut into her feet. She ran back to a safe distance a second time, but before long, the beauty of the jewel made her forget about the glass shards, so she walked on them again to get to the jewel.

This went on and on until the woman had lost all feeling in her feet. There she stood, marveling at the jewel while her numb feet rested on the sharp spikes of glass.

And she bled to death.

This graphic parable illustrates the insanity that sin inspires in us. We crave the very thing that eventually destroys us. And though we may see the danger at first, if we don't heed the warnings, our hearts soon become numb to sin's effects. Eventually we die, just like the woman in the parable.

For a biblical basis for this parable, read Romans 1:21-32 and Hebrews 3:12-13.

HOW TO CREATE YOUR OWN PARABLES

Creating parables is easy. All it requires is an understanding of the principle you wish to convey and a bit of imagination. Try following this simple outline for creating parables you can use with kids in your own small group.

Step 1: Choose a principle you want kids to learn. Choose something that can be expressed easily in one or two sentences. For example, "Unforgiveness makes your own heart sick."

Step 2: Think about things in life or situations that remind you of the principle. Sometimes this step can be made easier by simply brainstorming a list of all the things or situations that come to mind. Don't try to figure out how each thing you write might apply right now. Just get it all down on paper. For example, with the principle listed above, your list might look something like this:

Things	Situations
A Doctor	Man kills another's son,
Rocks in a river	the son's father wants to
A tree rotting inside out	take revenge, but ends up
Contagious disease	destroying himself.

Step 3: Test the ideas to come up with the best parable. In this case, a relational story or a comparison might work best. For example, "Unforgiveness is like a boy who gets a deep cut on his arm. The boy never cleans the wound, and it festers and becomes infected. If the boy never cleans it, his arm will eventually have to be cut off, or he will die."

Step 4: Personalize the story. Turn the parable into a full-fledged story or bring elements of your own life into it. This will make it more believable to kids and more meaningful to you.

 SAILING PARABLE

The kingdom of God is like a woman in a sailboat on a lake. If her sail and rudder are misaligned, she sits "dead in the water" regardless of how hard the wind blows. But with her rudder and sail correctly placed, the power of the wind carries her with joy across the waters and eventually leads her to the safety of the harbor.

In this parable the boat is the woman's life; the lake is the world. The sail represents faith, and the rudder represents the truth of God's Word. The wind is the power of God's Spirit. When faith and truth are correctly aligned, the woman moves through life with joy—not by her own power but by God's power. But if faith is misplaced, or the truth is not present, the woman's life becomes uncontrollable and "lost" at sea.

For the biblical basis for this parable, read John 3:5-8 and Zechariah 4:1-7.

ETERNAL-LIFE PARABLE

The kingdom of God is like the murderer who was brought before the righteous judge. The righteous judge pronounced the murderer guilty and sentenced him to death. Then to everyone's surprise (and without the murderer's request), the judge decreed that he would take the murderer's place in the electric chair so that the murderer would go free without cost. In addition, the judge rewrote his will and made the murderer the sole beneficiary of all his vast wealth.

This parable presents a striking picture of the depth of God's love expressed through Jesus on the cross. The judge represents both God the Father and the Son, and the man represents each of us. Not only did Jesus take the death penalty in our place, he also made us the inheritors of his glory.

For a biblical basis for this parable, read John 3:16 and Romans 5:6-21.

SLEEPING-FOOL PARABLE

There was once a fool who lived in a beautiful home next to a beautiful lake. Every day, he awoke very late in the day and spent his afternoons exploring the shore of the lake next to his home. Over time the fool became proud of his knowledge about the lake. He said to his soul, "Soul, you have become wise from all your years by the lake. Surely no one can tell you anything you haven't already learned on your own."

One day a young boy came up to the fool and greeted him kindly. Then the boy asked, "Did you see the swans fly in this morning? They were awesome!" (For early every morning, swans would fly in and rest on the water for a time before flying on.)

When the boy said this, the fool scoffed. "Boy," he said, "I've lived next to this lake all my life. There's no one alive who knows more about it than I do. And I can tell you with certainty that there are no swans here. You're just letting your imagination run away with you. You should stop telling lies and set your feet in reality."

At first the boy argued, saying, "No, no, but I saw them this morning!" But nothing he could say would convince the fool that the swans were real. Eventually, the boy gave up and walked away.

And the fool lived out his days believing there were no swans simply because he was too lazy to get up earlier and look.

This parable illustrates the foolish way many people reject the message of Christ. Because of their own life choices (the fool never rose early) and their subjective experiences (the fool had never seen the swans for himself), they conclude that the message of Christ is either false or powerless. The story illustrates how pride and arrogance are the dominant qualities that can keep us from God and cause us to live with a flawed, "small" perspective of the world.

For a biblical basis for this parable, read Proverbs 4:18-19; 28:26; and 2 Corinthians 4:3-4.

CHAPTER 4

TAKING TIME FOR PLAY

"The Son of Man came eating and drinking, and they say, 'Here is a glutton and a drunkard, a friend of tax collectors and "sinners." ' But wisdom is proved right by her actions."
—Matthew 11:19

Take a look at this quote by Robert Hotchkins, a theologian at the University of Chicago:

Christians ought to be celebrating constantly. We ought to be preoccupied with parties, banquets, feasts, and merriment. We ought to give ourselves over to veritable orgies of joy because we have been liberated from the fear of life and the fear of death. We ought to attract people to the church quite literally by the fun there is in being a Christian.[1]

What's your reaction to this quote? Suspicion? Defensiveness? Guilt? A combination of all three?

Of course, no one would argue that the Christian life is all fun and frivolity. If we're honest, we know the Christian life is fraught with trials, tests, and suffering that all work together to make us more like Jesus. Despite that understanding, there's often still a longing in all of us that asks quietly, "If Christ really has saved me, and if he now lives in me, shouldn't I be experiencing more joy than this?"

If you've ever asked that question, then the answer is unequivocally, "Yes, you should!"

We all lose sight of true joy at times. For some of us, the loss can last for years, even decades. But even if you lose your joy only from time to time, the causes for its departure are always the same. They are

● fear,

● worry, and

● habit.

If fear and worry don't steal your joy away, habit almost always will—that is, unless you choose to stop it.

Joy is more than just an emotion. It's a lifestyle attitude—a way of looking at life. Attitudes are largely the result of personal choices. So if you don't choose to have a joyful perspective about life, you probably never will.

Jesus chose to live in joy. He went to parties with sinners and probably knew how to laugh with the best of them. Perhaps it was that quality of joyfulness that made Jesus so offensive to the leaders of his day. Like many Christians today, the religious leaders of Jesus' day felt they needed to carry around a certain seriousness on their faces—mostly so the people around them would recognize how important they were and listen to their instructions as seriously as they dished them out.

Jesus wasn't that way. He broke the norm for a rabbi. He laughed. He enjoyed the company of common folk. He even played with children (despite his disciples' efforts to keep kids away from him). In short, *he had nothing to prove to anyone,* so he was free to play with all the fullness of his heart. Not in irreverence but in reverence. Not in mockery of his authority but in the absolute security of it.

As a small-group leader, you may be tempted to project an image to your kids of what you think they expect a leader to be: solemn, wise, always seriously pondering the mysteries of God and faith. But that's not the sort of leader Jesus was or is today. And that's not the sort of leader your intimate group needs to see either.

The childlike playfulness that comes from joy doesn't spontaneously erupt overnight. It requires vulnerability, trust, and a wonderful absence of self-awareness. In a small group like yours, kids have the rare opportunity to see more than just the polished teacher or confident counselor. They also have the chance to see genuine childlikeness, heartfelt laughter, and the immeasurable value of learning how to let go and simply have fun.

Choose joy for yourself every day. And open your life to let your small group watch you grow in your ability to play. You'll be amazed at how quickly they'll grow right along with you.

GROUP-APPLICATION IDEAS

To kick-start your group's play time, photocopy the "Dream Adventure Survey" (p. 61), and distribute it for your group members to fill out. Use kids' responses to start an Adventure-of-the-Month Club in which your small group comes together each month to participate in a fun adventure chosen by one of the group members.

In addition, use these other playful ideas to help your group learn how to embrace Christ's joy and fill their lives with childlike playfulness.

BIKE RIDE

Go on a sunrise bike ride. Make sure kids' bikes are mounted with head and tail lights. Ride your community's bike trails or explore less-traveled parts of the community.

CREATIVE MOTION

Make personalized skateboards, snowboards, or boogie boards. Go with kids to purchase the supplies you'll need from the hardware store and specialty shops, then work together on your personal creations. One week later, take your new toys out for a test run.

FORT FUN

Build a fort. Ask a landowner in your church to allow your kids use of some wooded land for a day. Have kids bring hammers, nails, saws, shovels, work gloves, and heavy twine. Use scrap wood around the area to construct the masterpiece. If it's winter and you live in a snowy region, build a snow fort or an igloo instead.

EXPLORATION

Explore a cave. Rather than just going on the guided tour, ask a caving expert to take your group to explore some of the less-traveled caves in your area.

GAMES GALORE

Check out these game book resources from Group Publishing: *Great Group Games for Youth Ministry; Low Cost, No Cost Ideas for Youth Ministry; Pick & Choose: Program Ideas for Youth Ministry; Boredom Busters; Have-a-Blast Games for Youth Groups; All-Star Games From All-Star Youth Leaders;* and *Quick Crowdbreakers and Games for Youth Groups.*

WHEELS

Go in-line skating. Have kids rent in-line skates from a local dealer, then take off for a fun tour of your community. If you feel really daring, get hockey sticks and play street hockey in your church parking lot. (Be sure kids have all the recommended pads and protection.)

CLOWNING

Go "clowning" in a hospital. Have kids spend a day getting decked out as clowns and visiting people in the hospital. Have them form teams of two or three to spread joy in the various wings of the hospital.

PERSONALITY COOKIES

Have a baking party. Use the cookie recipe below as the basis for a fun batch of "personality" cookies. Have group members create a list of people to make super-sized cookies for, then set aside enough dough to make a huge face of each person they've chosen. Send kids out to get decorating supplies such as nuts, berries, sprinkles, candy, and frosting. Then allow kids to create a personality cookie for each person on the list. Encourage group members to make the cookie look as much like the person as possible.

Once the cookies are done, deliver each cookie to the appropriate person along with a big hug.

PERSONALITY COOKIE RECIPE

½ cup butter	½ teaspoon vanilla
1 cup sugar	1½ cups flour
1 egg	1 teaspoon baking powder
1 tablespoon milk	¼ teaspoon salt

Mix all the ingredients, and form dough into large, flat cookies. Bake at 350 degrees for 12 to 15 minutes. Makes enough dough for two to three personality cookies.

TRIATHLON

Organize a recreational triathlon. Instead of competitive events such as running, biking, or swimming, choose "pure-fun" challenges such as volleyball, Frisbee golf, or horseshoes. Have church members form teams to join in the fun.

PEOPLE-POWER BOATS

Cosponsor a people-powered boat race in your community. Rally kids to get local businesses to sponsor a Crazy Boat Race. The only rules for construction are that each boat has to float and must be powered by human effort alone. Beyond that, anything goes. Have kids enter the race with their own creations. And be sure to require everyone to wear life jackets!

PARENTS DAY OUT

Sponsor a Parents Day Out. Have your group members spend a full afternoon looking after and playing with the children. Take them to an amusement park, a playground, or just into the backyard. Encourage teenagers to play right along with the children.

TREEHOUSE

Build a church treehouse. If you've got a large, sturdy oak tree or something similar on your church property, ask your church's permission to let your kids design and build a treehouse. Have kids design the treehouse so that it's unreachable by smaller children or other people in the neighborhood. (You can do this by making the ladder removable or by surrounding the house with a fence and a locked entry way.) Use the treehouse occasionally for group meetings or after-church devotions.

MOVIE MAGIC

Make a movie. Have group members design a remake of their favorite film or create a new plot altogether. Allow kids to cast themselves as characters. Then rent a camcorder for a day and shoot the movie. Watch it that night while enjoying popcorn together.

SING-ALONG

Go to karaoke night at the local teenage hangout. Many towns now have teen-only clubs that serve nonalcoholic beverages. If there's one in your area, find out which night it offers karaoke or an open mike. Then take your kids out for a night on the town. (Note: Most of these clubs will allow adults in if they're accompanied by teenagers.)

KITES

Go fly a kite. Take kids to Wal-Mart, Kmart, or some other discount store to buy inexpensive kites. Then head to the park for a day of kite-flying fun.

PICNIC CONTEST

Have a picnic contest. Form teams of two to three, and have teams compete to see who can put together the most spectacular, most unusual, or most visually stimulating picnic arrangement. Encourage teams to focus not just on food items but also on costumes and added decorations for their picnic settings.

COMMUNITY FUN

Venture into the community. Stay current on low-cost fun events in your community, such as art shows, outdoor plays, and concerts. When one comes along that looks interesting, gather your small group and join in the fun.

FLEA MARKET

Go to the flea market. Spend a morning with your group exploring the rarities you can find nowhere other than at these bastions of free enterprise. For added fun, go alone a day early and create a scavenger-type hunt for the excursion. Or ask kids to seek out rare items to use in decorating the youth room.

WALL PAINT

Finger-paint or splash-paint the walls of the youth room. Use drop cloths to cover the floors, windows, and anything else you don't want painted. Ask your local paint shop to donate bright-colored paints for your group to use. Once you've got all the supplies, let kids go at it.

FULL-MOON HIKE

Go on a full-moon hike in the woods. Then tell "God" stories (instead of ghost stories) around a campfire while you roast marshmallows.

T-SHIRT CREATION

Design and create personalized T-shirts from scratch. The next time your local fabric store has a clearance sale, pile the group into a van and go for a visit. Have kids purchase material and T-shirt patterns for creating personalized T-shirts. Kids can use as many different materials as they wish for their creations. Once you've collected all the needed supplies, go to a young person's home and work together to assemble your creations. If you have an especially daring group, have them go out on the town together that night while modeling their new wardrobe.

DREAM ADVENTURE SURVEY

In the space below, write a description of one or two crazy, daring, or fun adventurous things you'd like to do sometime but never have. Make sure your adventures aren't too expensive and can be done within a sixty-mile radius of your community.

_____

_____

_____

_____

_____

_____

_____

_____

_____

_____

_____

_____

_____

_____

_____

_____

_____

_____

_____

_____

_____

_____

_____

_____

Endnote

1. Brennan Manning, *The Ragamuffin Gospel* (Portland, OR: Multnomah Books, 1990), 149.

CHAPTER 5

TAKING TIME FOR REST

"The apostles gathered around Jesus and reported to him all they had done and taught. Then, because so many people were coming and going that they did not even have a chance to eat, he said to them, 'Come with me by yourselves to a quiet place and get some rest.' So they went away by themselves in a boat to a solitary place."

—Mark 6:30-32

Have you ever wondered why God created us with the need for sleep? Why not create us so we could keep going twenty-four hours a day? Wouldn't we learn more in a lifetime that way? Wouldn't we be able to accomplish more and serve God more effectively?

If we stop to think about it, we'll find there's a lesson for us in everything God does. In the physical realm, rest is a time each day when we tune out what's going on around us and allow our bodies to release the pressures of the day. It's a time to restore our bodies to full strength. When we're injured, most of our healing happens while we rest. And rest time is also when we dream.

The spiritual parallels are obvious, though most Christians rarely heed them. God believed rest was so important that he made it a law under the old covenant. The writer of Hebrews was also adamant when he wrote, "There remains, then, a Sabbath-rest for the people of God; for anyone who enters God's rest also rests from his own work, just as God did from his. Let us, therefore, make every effort to enter that rest, so that no one will fall by following [the Israelites'] example of disobedience" (Hebrews 4:9-11).

According to this passage, rest isn't just something you do; it's a continual state of being—a full-time way of life for Christians who believe.

No doubt that's why Jesus placed such a premium on rest. Not only did he regularly go off alone to private, restful places (more on that in Chapter 7), but he encouraged his disciples to do the same. He even seemed to live in a state of "deliberate unhurriedness." In John 11, when Jesus learned that his friend Lazarus was dying, did he drop everything and rush to his side? No. John's account tells us that "when he heard that Lazarus was sick, he stayed where he was two more days" (John 11:6). How different that is from some of us whose lives can sometimes be described as an endless string of reactions to the crises we continually encounter.

But not Jesus. He rested in the guiding power of the Holy Spirit. He rested in the knowledge that his heavenly Father was in control, so he didn't have to be. Jesus knew how to rest.

As a small-group leader, modeling and teaching rest to your group members may be one of the most challenging tasks you'll ever face. But it also can be one of the most rewarding. You have a luxury that most leaders in larger groups never have—you can spend creative "downtime" with your group members. That's nearly impossible to do with a whole group of fifty or one hundred kids. But it's ideal for small groups.

Even so, your kids might not understand the value of restful activities at first. That's OK. After all, they've been raised in a world that says "living" means going full-throttle twenty-four hours a day. Give them time to see how the Christian life offers a better way to live—a way that's full of excitement *and* rest, adventure *and* peace.

Read over the restful ideas highlighted in the pages that follow. Pay special attention to those ideas that focus on your personal life. You can talk about rest all you want with your small group, but if you don't model it, they won't really listen. Let them see the fruit of rest in your life, and help them understand how true rest can be fun, invigorating, and far from boring.

GROUP-APPLICATION IDEAS

Use these ideas to develop a heart of rest in your own life and guide kids toward understanding the value of rest in their day-to-day lives.

CHINESE-FOOD-AND-MOVIE NIGHT

When choosing to rest, sometimes the easiest option is also the best. On an evening when you want to just relax and lock the world outside, invite your group members over for a video night. Rent a relaxing or funny movie, and have kids pitch in to get Chinese food delivered to your home. Once the food arrives, turn out the lights, spread

TIP BOX
If kids aren't in the mood for a movie, play cards or board games instead. And don't force group discussion about the event. Rest becomes work when kids are forced to think through the theological implications of their restful activity. Save the discussions for another time.

out the pillows, and watch the movie while you enjoy your favorite Chinese dishes.

DAY OF SILENCE

This challenging activity can be done one of two ways. One way is to set aside a special weekend day when kids can arrange to free up their schedules for a full twelve-hour period.

On that day, gather group members together and explain the day's planned events. For example, you could go to the mall, go out to eat together, go see a movie, go for a hike, participate in a scavenger hunt, or play games together. The only catch is that for the entire day, kids are not allowed to speak at all. All communication must be nonverbal or written. In addition, kids are not allowed to explain to any "outside" people why they aren't talking.

After you've explained the day's events, start your silent day together.

The other way to do this activity is to provide a sheet for kids to sign up for silent days they choose on their own. Kids may join in pairs or threesomes to share their silent days together, or they may spend the time alone. On their assigned days, kids may do anything they wish, but they may not speak to anyone for any reason all day long.

Once kids have experienced a day of silence, either together or alone, gather everyone together and ask:

● **How did not speaking affect the people around you?**

● **How did it affect you?**

● **What unexpected good things came out of your experience?**

● **What was the hardest thing about your day of silence?**

Read aloud Psalm 46:10-11. Then ask:

● **Did being silent increase your sense of peace overall? Why or why not?**

● **How does "resting our mouths" increase our awareness of God in the world?**

● **What has this experience taught you about rest?**

ELECTRONIC-MEDIA FAST

Here's a challenging way to get your group members to experience more rest in their lives. For one full week, ask kids to agree to a full electronic-media fast. That means no television, no music, no computer games, no Internet, no video games, and no movies for seven days. With all their extra time, encourage group members to read novels, draw or paint, or work on some type of craft or mechanical projects. Also encourage them to spend regular time in Bible study and prayer.

At the end of the fast, gather kids together for a debriefing. Ask:

● **What was the hardest thing about your fast?**

● **What surprised you the most about this experience?**

● **What sorts of things did you do with your extra time?**

● **How do you feel about your experience now that it's over?**

● **Would you do something like this again? Why or why not?**

Read aloud Luke 10:38-42. Ask:

● **How do we tend to be like Martha in this account?** (We're always doing something; we feel the need to keep busy; our schedules are full.)

● **In what ways was our media fast like Mary in this story?** (Mary knew what was most important to focus on; when we move away from the busyness of our lives, we can focus on God.)

● **What have you gained from this experience that you'll apply to your life from now on?**

LOCAL-SIGHTSEEING DAY

Ever wonder what other people come to see when they visit your community? Why not find out? Take group members out for a slow-paced day of seeing the sights in your area. Plan a full day of events. Start with a visit to a local county, state, or national park, then move on to museums, zoos, or any well-known industries that offer tours for visitors. Conclude your day with a trip to a local theme park, sporting event, or popular restaurant.

For added fun, have kids take along cameras to chronicle the day's events, then use their photos to create a memory-board mural in your meeting room. Kids will be surprised by all there is to do in your area, and they'll learn a little history in the process.

LOW-KEY GETAWAY

As a real shock to your kids' systems, plan a low-key retreat that's designed to be restful. For example, arrange to rent a time-share condo in the mountains or on a lake near your community for one week (or a weekend). Stock up on provisions and supplies as you would for any other extended trip with kids. But *plan nothing* except a worship time and Bible study each day. Leave kids' schedules totally free to do as much or as little as they wish. Set no schedule for waking or sleeping; instead, limit your schedule requirements to meal times and Bible study times each day.

Before the getaway, make sure kids understand the nature of the retreat and the fact that, although they'll be free to do what they wish, they'll be secluded away from any major concentrations of people or businesses. Encourage kids to bring things with them they'd like to work on, such as books or personal projects.

During the retreat, take kids through a biblical study of rest. Use passages such as Hebrews 4, Mark 6, Isaiah 58, and Exodus 20 as a basis for talking about what biblical rest is and why it is such a vital aspect of the Christian life. Challenge kids to make "entering God's rest" a personal goal for their lives.

MASSAGE-SCHOOL VISIT

Many cities have massage-therapy schools or colleges offering degrees in physical therapy or massage therapy. Arrange for a massage class to host a visit by your small group for a special lab time. Many massage-class instructors will welcome the opportunity to have fresh subjects for their class members to practice on. And the massage will be a relaxing gift for your group members.

MOVIE-MARATHON DAY

Not all vacations have to be costly. You can take kids on a one-day vacation without ever leaving your home—by having a Movie-Marathon Day.

Have kids help prepare enough food for the whole day, then join you in your home for a relaxing mental excursion via your VCR. Spend a day watching movies your group members will enjoy. For example, the seven-hour saga *Anne of Green Gables* and *Anne of Avonlea* works great for a group of girls, while a marathon viewing of the *Star Wars* trilogy might work well for a group of guys.

TIP BOX
An adventurous variation on this activity is to rent a video game machine and play video games all day. Of course, you'll want to avoid violent games. Instead, choose long-lasting adventure games. These games usually take a main character on some type of noble quest. They're fun because everyone can participate, and they're more interactive than the beat-em-up-type games.

If your group includes both guys and girls, choose movies according to categories such as comedies, dramas, action thrillers, or movies that feature a favorite actor. It's always a good idea to preview the movies so you can replace those with inappropriate scenes or language.

Another fun idea is to watch a day's worth of Laurel and Hardy or Bugs Bunny shorts. Whatever movies you choose, be sure to provide lots of popcorn and drinks.

PERSONAL-REST SCHEDULE

Many people don't have time for rest because their schedules don't allow for it. The solution: Change your schedule to include regular, nonnegotiable rest times.

How much rest time should you schedule? Preferences will vary from person to person, but for someone in full-time ministry, here's a good rule of thumb to follow:

One hour of rest each day,
One day of rest each week,
One weekend of rest each month,
One week of rest each year.

In this equation, rest doesn't mean working on something other than small-group ministry or going on stressful, action-filled vacations. It means rest.

During your rest times, follow Jesus' example and make yourself unavailable to the outside world. Don't answer the phone (remember, it's there for your convenience—not the other way around). In fact, if possible, don't even stay home where people can find you. Spend your time away in the woods, in a friend's empty home, or even in a hotel.

If you have trouble justifying resting when "there's so much to be done," try thinking of rest time as your "date with God." If you do, you may be less likely to treat that time as optional or waste it in lazy ways.

Then help your small-group members create their own personal rest schedules patterned after your own but tailored to their situations.

POETRY BY FIRE

Take kids out at night to a secluded place where campfires are allowed. Ask kids to bring books of poetry or short stories they enjoy. Have kids build a fire while you prepare hot dogs on sticks for group members to roast. While the group enjoys the hot dogs, ask individuals to take turns reading aloud poems or short stories they're willing to share. Continue until everyone has had a chance to read at least four times.

As a relaxing ending to the experience, put out the fire and ask kids to lie down on their backs and watch the stars for a while. If kids want to talk while they're watching the stars, ask them to speak using only sentences that rhyme in honor of the evening's poetic theme.

TIP BOX

Not everyone in your group may enjoy reading literature. If that's so, don't pressure all your group members to join you for this event. Encourage those who enjoy literature to come, and tell the others that you'll plan a special rest event with them on a later date.

WEEKEND WILDERNESS WALK

Nature generally has a natural calming effect on people. To help kids experience the rest that the outdoors can bring, take them on a wilderness walk. Choose a wooded trail that's not too difficult but is long enough for at least a three-hour hike. Before you leave, make sure kids each have adequate shoes and water for the trail.

While you walk, keep talking to a minimum. Instead, encourage kids to focus on the world around them. Ask them to test the limits of their senses by trying to be aware of every sight, smell, and sound.

After the hike, stop at a local fast-food restaurant for beverages. Ask

TIP BOX

If you have more than one day available to you and your group, consider extending the hike into a wilderness-weekend backpacking trip. Most state and national parks have well-marked trails and campsites available for groups who want to hike several days into the wilderness. Ask an experienced backpacker to help with supplies for you and your group members. Then take off for a few days of rest in the woods.

kids to compare how they felt at the beginning of the hike with their feelings during the hike and when the hike ended. Then ask:

● **How does your experience on the trail compare with what you're experiencing around you right now?**

● Why do you think people surround themselves with such activity all the time?

● Do you think taking time to rest, like we did today, is important in life? Why or why not?

● What are your favorite ways to rest?

● What are ways we can develop an attitude of rest in our lives?

● What other things could we do as a group to develop our ability to rest in God?

CHAPTER 6

REACHING OUT TO THE WORLD

"These twelve Jesus sent out with the following instructions...'As you go, preach this message: The kingdom of heaven is near. Heal the sick, raise the dead, cleanse those who have leprosy, drive out demons. Freely you have received, freely give...He who receives you receives me, and he who receives me receives the one who sent me. Anyone who receives a prophet because he is a prophet will receive a prophet's reward, and anyone who receives a righteous man because he is a right-eous man will receive a righteous man's reward. And if anyone gives even a cup of cold water to one of these little ones because he is my dis-ciple, I tell you the truth, he will cer-tainly not lose his reward.' "

—Matthew 10:5, 7-8, 40-42

There's no doubt that the practice of Christian outreach has been abused by religious groups over the years. Approach just about any person on the street and ask what images come to mind when you say "evangelism" or "Christian outreach," and he or she will most likely describe to you the same image you're picturing now: a man or woman dressed in black, shaking a huge Bible in your face—or worse, hitting you over the head with it.

Bible thumpers, we're sometimes called. And maybe the name isn't as misplaced as we'd like to think. Sure, few of us have ever assaulted anyone with a Bible, but sometimes a condescending frown, a glare, or a judgmental "humph" can do just as much damage. Even the way we distance ourselves from "worldly" people sends a message of condemnation far louder than the "thump, thump" of a Bible.

But wait a minute! Isn't it right that we distance ourselves? How else can we keep away from temptation and avoid all "appearance of evil"?

Of course, we should avoid temptations that could cause us to fall into sin. But too often, this line of reasoning is used only as a smoke screen to hide the real reason we isolate ourselves from the grittier sides of reality: We simply don't feel comfortable.

The truth is that genuine outreach isn't just uncomfortable—it's dangerous. Jesus told his disciples, "I am sending you out like sheep among wolves. Therefore be as shrewd as snakes and as innocent as doves" (Matthew 10:16). Remember, this is what *Jesus* says about the nature of outreach. From his words, we can see we have good reason to feel uncomfortable or even threatened. Songwriter Wayne Watson describes the situation this way: "There's a fine line between taking bread with a lost man, and being consumed by his ways while reaching out in love."

Despite the discomfort and danger that comes with genuine outreach, Jesus did it all the time. And he sent out his disciples to do the same. But he didn't do it to add members to his congregation, condemn nonbelievers, or make himself look righteous in the eyes of others. Jesus did it for one reason alone—the *only* reason any outreach of any kind should ever be attempted.

That reason? Love.

With love as your sole motivation, outreach literally becomes an act of love:

Not an attempt to increase attendance on Sundays.

Not a vehicle for condemning people for their sin.

Not a way to win an argument with a non-Christian.

And certainly not a way to "score points" with God.

That's why Jesus could say that outreach encompasses a much larger scope than just telling others about the message of the Gospel (although that is the most important aspect of genuine outreach). It involves *living out* the Gospel's message—meeting people's real needs, sharing our lives with them, even serving them with something as simple as a cold glass of water on a hot day.

Genuine outreach is a vital aspect of our faith in Jesus. It's also a vital contributor to the health of any small group. Without a loving "outward" focus, small groups tend to become ingrown, isolated, and judgmental of those on the outside. Just like Jesus' original disciples, your group members need to learn how to reach out to others regularly. They need to discover that genuine outreach isn't about getting another notch on their Bibles. It's about learning the value and life-changing power of genuine, unconditional love.

GROUP-APPLICATION IDEAS

You can help the members of your small group learn this important lesson for themselves. And in the process, they can learn to become more like Jesus. Use these ideas to help them reach out to others in creative, loving ways.

ADOPT A FRIEND

Each semester or quarter in school, have each group member find a non-Christian friend to adopt as his or her own personal servant project. Have group members make it their aim to serve their special people for the entire semester or quarter in any way they can. For example, group members could include their friends in church events or

TIP BOX

Although the primary purpose of this activity isn't to convert people to Christianity, don't be surprised if several of your group members' adopted friends become followers of Christ and full-time members of your small group.

other activities that might interest them. They could also help their adopted friends by studying with them, eating lunch with them, or just listening to their problems. And, of course, group members can pray for their friends throughout the year.

CELEBRATION-OF-FAITH PARTY

This courageous idea provides a great way for your group members to tell their friends about their faith in God. Have group members invite their non-Christian friends from school and work to a party at one of your young people's homes. Make "celebration" the focus of the party, with lots of fun food and drinks and (if possible) live music. Let group members mingle freely with their guests and get to know each other's friends.

At some point during the evening, call everyone together and have group members explain that the reason they organized this party is to celebrate their relationship with Jesus—and that they wanted to share their joy with their friends from school and work.

After this general explanation, have each group member tell about his or her own relationship with God and how it has brought a new perspective and joy to life. Encourage kids to keep their talks short so everyone can have equal time. Once kids have finished sharing about their relationships with God, have them thank their friends for listening. Then serve food and beverages and return to the celebration.

TIP BOX

Too often, activities of this sort can be turned into manipulative events in which guests can feel they've been tricked into coming just so someone can pressure them to become Christians.

Avoid this situation by encouraging group members to see that the goal of the party is simply to share with their friends about something they care about, not to convince them to become Christians on the spot. After kids share their faith stories, encourage them to personally thank each person for coming and for listening to them. In addition, advise kids not to discuss their faith with anyone further that evening unless someone asks.

LETTERS

Have each group member create a list of ten people he or she has never met but admires greatly. These people may include actors, social activists, religious or political figures, or professional athletes.

Once kids' lists are complete, compile all their responses into one list. Have kids write a letter to each of their favorite people, telling them two things:

- what the group member admires about him or her, and
- how the group member's faith in God has impacted his or her life.

Allow kids a week or two to complete their letters. (Each person can write just one main letter and adjust it as needed for each person on the list.) Have kids research addresses for all the people on their lists.

When kids have finished their letters, collect them and prepare them for mailing. But before you send them off, call kids together to pray for the people they're writing to, that God will use their letters to positively influence these people toward God.

MAP PRAYER-TOUR

Get a street map of your community, and post it on a bulletin board in your group's meeting room. Have kids place push-pins on the map at locations where their "friends with needs" live. Once the map is fully marked, have group members spend time each week standing around the map and praying for individual kids whose homes are marked. Encourage group members to stay updated on their friends' needs so the group can pray more effectively for them.

For every answered prayer, place a small ribbon under the pushpin marking the appropriate person's home. When the map gets too full of ribbons to be used effectively, have a Praise Party during your regular meeting time to thank God for answers to prayers. Music, beverages, and treats can add to the festivities. Then put up a new community map and start the process again.

PEER COUNSELING HOT LINE

In a small group, you have the advantage of being able to train kids more intensively. One way to take advantage of this fact is to take kids through an extensive peer-counseling course. You'll find peer-counseling training programs at your local Christian bookstore. Or you can contact a counselor in your church or at a local Christian clinic to provide training.

After taking kids through the course, set up a community-wide crisis hot line from your church. Rather than having the hot line operate twenty-four hours a day, advertise special times when the hot line will be in operation. For example, run the hot line only during certain times of the week, such as Friday and Saturday nights. Or run the hot line only during particular times of the year, such as during finals and major holidays.

Encourage kids to use their skills to guide their peers toward positive choices and, if possible, toward faith in God.

TIP BOX

Even with extensive training, there are some situations your group members shouldn't try to handle. For those situations, find one or two qualified Christian counselors you can recommend to people over the phone. If possible, ask at least one Christian counselor to work with your group on an on-call basis. That way, in case of an emergency (such as a suicidal caller), you'll have easy access to a professional counselor. Also provide kids with numbers for both the police and the fire department in case the need arises to call them.

SLICE-OF-LIFE DRAMA

Slice-of-Life dramas are unannounced, interactive skits about real life that are performed in public places. Unannounced means the skits start suddenly with no introduction. Interactive means that the actors and the observers often converse throughout the drama, so much so that many observers may not realize the performance is a skit until it's over.

These types of dramas work best in open shopping areas, such as street malls and flea markets. The goal of these dramas is to entertain and to introduce topics for later thought or discussion with the actors.

Here's an example of how a slice-of-life drama might work: On a busy street mall, a couple (two actors) are walking arm in arm along with the crowd. Suddenly, the girl breaks free of the guy's arm and yells, "I don't care what you think! If I want to wear them, I'm going to wear them!" (The drama has now begun.)

The girl pulls a pair of bunny ears out of her coat and slips them on her head.

"C'mon, Michelle, you look ridiculous," says the guy. "It's embarrassing."

"I do not look ridiculous," retorts Michelle. "I'm expressing my individuality. And if you can't embrace my uniqueness, it just shows that you're shallow."

"Michelle," he says, looking around. "People are watching us."

"Let 'em watch," yells Michelle. She turns to face the crowd. "What do you think?" she asks. "Shouldn't a person be allowed to do anything she wants, as long as she thinks it's OK for her?"

However the crowd responds, Michelle then goes on to assert that anyone can do anything he or she wants, as long as it seems right to that person. From there, the skit could go any number of directions. The guy (let's call him Matt) could argue that there are some things that are absolute wrongs, no matter what people think about them—such as murder, drug abuse, or physical abuse in a relationship.

TIP BOX

If your group members aren't interested in drama, try the same approach by having small groups of kids form performance groups—singers, guitarists, clowns, or mimes—and stage performances on street malls or in other public places. If it seems appropriate, have kids share their faith stories with the audience between performances.

Because the skits are interactive, be careful not to make your dramas too shocking for audiences to handle. For example, in a "staged" skit like the one above, Matt might pull out a fake gun and point it at Michelle as a dramatic way to demonstrate the absolute wrongness of some acts. In an "unstaged" interactive drama, however, this would be totally inappropriate and even dangerous. Not everyone may realize your drama is just a skit, and people may react as though the situation—and the gun—are real.

The skit could end with Matt quoting a passage from the Bible or putting on a pair of mouse ears. The goal is not so much to give answers as it is to raise questions—questions that can then be discussed privately with the actors or just pondered in a way that gives the Holy Spirit an opportunity to work in people's hearts.

After you've explained the concept to your small-group members, have them create skits based on real-life issues they know people struggle with. Encourage kids to make the skits entertaining as well as provocative. Prepare three or four skits that can be used anywhere, any time. Then take kids to the open market or a street mall for the day and release them to entertain the crowds.

After the event, gather kids together to have them tell each other about their experiences with the people they encountered. Pray together that God's Spirit will prompt their observers to look for answers in the Bible or that they might ask Christians they know.

 FAITH-STORY BOOK

After leading kids through a study on sharing their faith, have kids write out their personal stories of how God has changed them and influenced their lives. Collect kids' stories and compile them together into a reproducible booklet. Then, as part of a welcome packet for visiting teenagers, include the faith-story book. This is a powerful way for kids to share their faith with everyone who visits your small group.

TIP BOX
As gifts for graduating seniors, frame kids' testimonies and present them to students as special going-away presents and as encouragement to keep growing in their relationships with God.

As new kids join your group, add their written faith stories to the booklet.

VOLUNTEER TEAM

Your kids are well equipped to become an effective volunteer team for several volunteer organizations in your community. With a little training, your entire group could volunteer to work with terminal patients, Habitat for Humanity, or the Special Olympics, as well as any youth organizations.

As your group members serve others in their community, they'll form new relationships that can lead to natural opportunities for sharing their faith. But even if no verbal sharing occurs, serving the community is still a great way to demonstrate the love of Jesus to others.

SMALL-GROUP BLESSING FUND

Most kids in your group can name several people they know who are struggling financially or who have specific financial needs. Establish a special blessing fund with a combination of these ideas: (1) ask your church's permission to earmark a small percentage of the church budget for a blessing fund that the group can draw from to give to people in need, (2) conduct a fund-raiser dedicated to funding this project, and (3) encourage young people to personally contribute to the fund.

Encourage kids to be attentive to the needs of people around them and to talk about those needs with the whole group when you meet together. Then, each month or so, have group members decide together how to use the money to most effectively help meet the needs of the people they've encountered.

CHAPTER 7

SEEKING GOD IN PRAYER

"And when you pray, do not be like the hypocrites, for they love to pray standing in the synagogues and on the street corners to be seen by men. I tell you the truth, they have received their reward in full. But when you pray, go into your room, close the door and pray to your Father, who is unseen. Then your Father, who sees what is done in secret, will reward you."

—Matthew 6:5-6

Jesus always lived what he taught. Every teaching he gave concerning prayer can be seen reflected in his own prayer life during his ministry on earth. And because he believed in the *private* nature of prayer, we know relatively little about Jesus' prayer life during his time on earth. We don't know, for example, what he typically prayed about, how he expressed his prayers, or how God typically responded to him. What we do know from Scripture is that Jesus prayed often, usually in solitude, and that his prayers sometimes lasted all night.

Several Gospels refer to Jesus going off alone to pray. Since he didn't usually have a room to pray in, he often chose a mountainside. Although what went on during those extended encounters with God is largely a mystery to us—just as it was to his disciples at the time—we can draw some conclusions based on the context of those private experiences.

For example, Jesus spent a whole night in prayer before he chose the twelve apostles (Luke 6:12). His experience of walking on water occurred after a long prayer session (Matthew 14:23). On one occasion, he chose to move his ministry to another part of the country after spending time in prayer (Mark 1:35).

Jesus considered prayer an essential foundation to everything he did on earth. Perhaps Luke expressed this quality best when he made this observation about Jesus in Luke 5:15-16: "The news about him spread all the more, so that crowds of people came to hear him and to be healed of their sicknesses. *But Jesus often withdrew to lonely places and prayed.*"

For Jesus, prayer was far more than a spiritual request box or a cosmic battery recharger. Prayer was the avenue for communion with his greatest love—his heavenly Father. And, in a mysterious way, it was also his one connection with his own true identity. Prayer provided Jesus with guidance, not only about what to do in life but also about who he was.

We see this aspect of Jesus' prayer life illustrated in the account of Christ's transfiguration (Luke 9:28-36). At a time when Jesus was about to enter his darkest hour on earth, he went off to pray, this time taking a few of the disciples with him. During his prayer, Moses and Elijah appeared to encourage him about his future, and God himself reaffirmed that Jesus was his true Son.

As God's adopted children, prayer is as vital to our lives as it was to Christ's. As with Jesus, prayer provides us with a vital connection to our greatest love—our Father in heaven. It provides us with guidance about what to do in life; and, like Jesus, prayer even provides us with understanding about our true identities. (See Colossians 3:1-3.) Prayer is our lifeline to God. Without it, our spiritual lives will die.

Prayer was not only vital to Jesus' ministry on earth; it was probably one of his greatest joys. You can make it one of yours as well and help your kids discover the truth: that real life is found in only one place—God's presence.

As a leader of a small group, you have the opportunity to follow Jesus' example in making prayer a central part of your ministry with kids. Being like Jesus in this area involves more "modeling" of true prayer than directly teaching kids about it. That's why many of the activities suggested in this chapter focus on developing your own prayer life apart from your group. But there are also opportunities for you to help your kids develop their prayer lives more effectively.

Jesus never harped on the disciples' need to pray. Instead, the way he modeled prayer in front of them caused them to take interest (see Luke 11:1). You can use the same approach with your group members. As they watch the life that comes from your own prayer time with God, you will pique their interest to learn more. Then, as their interest grows, you can use the following activities to help them learn about developing their own connection with God.

GROUP-APPLICATION IDEAS

Use these ideas to help you and your kids develop an authentic prayer life with God.

B.I.P. 'N' S.I.P.

Set up a prayer covenant program called B.I.P. 'n' S.I.P. (Brothers in Prayer and Sisters in Prayer). Explain to group members that B.I.P. 'n' S.I.P. is a program in which pairs of kids voluntarily enter into friendship prayer covenants with each other. These prayer covenants require kids to know what's happening in their partners' lives and to pray regularly together for each other's needs.

Initially, set up the covenants to last six weeks. If kids' interest continues to grow, allow them to form new B.I.P. 'n' S.I.P. covenants that last up to sixteen weeks. During their covenant time, partners must pray together at least once a week and must pray for their partners on their own at least one other time during the week.

Here's a B.I.P. 'n' S.I.P. covenant commitment card you can use with your group members:

B.I.P. 'N' S.I.P. COVENANT

Partner #1 _____

Partner #2 _____

On this date, _____, we agree to enter

into a covenant together as prayer partners for the

next _____ weeks. During the duration of our

covenant, we commit to do the following things:

• update each other at least once a week about

the events in our lives and how those events are

affecting us,

• pray together at least once a week for each oth-

er's needs, and

• pray separately for each other's needs at least

once a week.

"BODY-NEEDS" PRAYER EVENT

Have your group members sponsor a forty-eight-hour, church-wide body-needs prayer event. Two or three Sunday mornings in a row, distribute index cards during the morning service, and ask congregation members to write on the cards any requests they have that they'd like the church to pray for. Requests may be anonymous, and any number of requests may be turned in by one person. Ask church members to include only one request on each card they turn in.

Once all the cards are collected, set the dates for a forty-eight-hour, continuous body-needs prayer event, with thirty-minute time slots people can volunteer to fill. Encourage your group members to fill as many of the slots as they can themselves.

If your church doesn't have a designated prayer room, set up a specific room to use for this purpose during the event. In the prayer room, place the cards that people filled out with requests for prayer.

As people come to pray, have them pray about the requests listed on the cards one at a time. Ask participants to place a check mark next to each request they pray for. Encourage people to pray through the entire list of requests before going back to pray for items that already have been covered.

After the prayer event, set aside time in a morning service for church members to share any results that came out of the prayer time. Also encourage your group members to share with the congregation what they learned from the experience.

MIRACLE MAN

Take group members through a study of Jesus' miracles as recorded in the four Gospels. Form investigative teams of two or three, and assign each team a different set of miracles to

study. For each miracle, ask these questions:
- **What was the circumstance Jesus faced?**
- **What miracle did Jesus perform?**
- **How did he perform the miracle?**
- **What might have been his motivation for performing this miracle?**

For your convenience, here's a reference list of many of the miracles of Jesus recorded in the Gospels:

Healings	Command over nature	Bringing the dead to life
Matthew 8:2-4 Matthew 8:5-13 Matthew 8:14-15 Matthew 8:28-34 Matthew 9:32-33 Mark 1:23-26 Mark 2:3-12 Mark 5:25-29 Mark 7:24-30 Mark 7:31-37 Mark 8:22-26 Luke 6:6-10 Luke 9:38-43 Luke 11:14 Luke 13:11-13 Luke 14:1-4 Luke 17:11-19 Luke 18:35-43 Luke 22:50-51 John 4:46-54 John 5:1-9 John 9:1-7	Matthew 8:23-27 Matthew 15:32-38 Matthew 17:24-27 Mark 6:48-51 Mark 11:12-14, 20-25 Luke 5:4-11 Luke 9:12-17 John 2:1-11 John 21:1-11	Matthew 9:18-19, 23-25 Luke 7:11-15 John 11:1-44

When teams have investigated their assigned miracles, have them report their findings to the whole group. Jesus never did a miracle without a reason, so be sure kids discuss Jesus' motivation for performing miracles in each situation. Close by asking:
- **How does understanding Jesus' motivation for performing miracles help us discern why God does or doesn't perform miracles today?**

ONE-DAY PRAYER RETREAT

Set aside a full day for a group prayer retreat. Before the retreat, meet with individuals in your group, and help them design their own personal days of prayer. Help them design special handouts to work through or short projects they can do on their own during the retreat to help them develop their prayer lives. Have kids keep journals of their experiences during the day.

Also schedule corporate prayer times during the one-day retreat, such as singing prayerful songs together or praying about specific issues as a group.

The best setting for this retreat is outdoors in a wooded state park. If a location like that isn't possible for your group, take kids to a church member's lake-side house or even to a ranch location. Wherever you go, make sure kids are able to spread out away from each other and that they also have a place to gather together.

After the one-day retreat, have kids come together to share their experiences. Then ask:

- **What did you enjoy about this experience?**
- **What was difficult about this experience?**
- **What would you do differently if you could do this again?**
- **What were your concerns about this experience before it began?**
- **What did God reveal to you in your prayer experience today?**
- **Do you feel like you met with God? Why or why not?**
- **When we pray, how do we know we're getting through?**
- **Jesus spent a lot of time alone with God, just as we did today. How do you suppose he benefited from those experiences?**
- **What hindrances or distractions sometimes keep us from communing with God the way Jesus did?**
- **What can we do this week to improve our connection with God?**

PATIENT PRAYER

Working with a local hospital chaplain, arrange a time for group members to visit patients and pray for their needs. Have young people form groups of three or four (including an adult volunteer) so none of the patients will feel overwhelmed. Have the adult volunteers guide kids in asking the patients about their illnesses, injuries, and other needs. Then pray together as a group.

Also have teenagers visit, pray for, and encourage church members who are shut-in, injured, or ill.

PERSON OF THE WEEK

Each week assign one person in your group to be the group's prayer focus for the week. During your regular small-group meeting, have the person of the week share all the prayer requests he or she would like the group to pray for in the coming week. Encourage kids to voice both "external" and "internal" requests. For example, "I need God's help to write my English paper" (external request), and "I need to be more patient with my little sister" (internal request).

Once the requests are made, have kids pray together for the person of the week. Then encourage kids to pray for that person all week long, at least once every day. Having a person of the week for kids to pray for helps kids feel more comfortable telling others about their needs. And it encourages group members to pray for each other.

TIP BOX
Make sure you include yourself as the person of the week from time to time.

PERSONAL PRAYER RETREATS

As a part of your regular schedule at the church, set aside a specific amount of time every six months for your own personal prayer retreat.

Plan the retreat as you would a retreat for your small group, complete with a special location, a theme, and a schedule of activities. Create special work sheets and one-person projects for yourself to help in your prayer time. For example, as a part of your retreat you could study the prayers recorded in the Bible or study a book about prayer, such as *Daring to Draw Near* by John White (InterVarsity Press) or *If Ye Shall Ask* by Oswald Chambers (Zondervan Publishing House).

In your personal schedule include meal times (unless you're fasting), free time, and times for rising and going to bed. If there's sightseeing you'd like to do, schedule it in as well. But set aside the majority of your time for purposeful, directed prayer. Keep a journal of all your prayer sessions for future reference.

TIP BOX
As a cost cutter for your personal retreat, consider packing a cot and staying in a church for your retreat location. Many churches have showers and rooms suitable for sleeping. Call the churches in the area where you'd like to go and explain to them your reason for coming. Most churches will be glad to take you in for a few days.

PRAYER RECORD

In a three-ring binder, create an ongoing record of your intercession for each young person in your small group. See the "Prayer Record" on page 92 for an idea of how you might organize your record. Pray for one group member each week, then repeat the list through the year.

On the record, include group members' specific prayer requests, insights

TIP BOX
As a special gift to group members, consider binding their intercessory records and presenting them as gifts at graduation. It's a great way for them to see how God has worked in their lives. ➔

However, if you decide to do this, make sure you keep your intercessory records both encouraging and legible!

——————————————

you have about each group member's needs, and a detailed account of what you pray for and how God answers. Add on additional pages for each group member as needed.

PRAYER RECORD

Name _____

Date _____

Requests _____

_____

_____

_____

My Insights_____

_____

_____

_____

My Prayer/God's Response _____

_____

_____

_____

PRAYER WALKS

Sensitize your group members to the need for intercession by taking them on prayer walks through various areas in your community. Walk through downtown areas, college campuses, or various neighborhoods, and pray as you go.

Provide kids with a prayer list to help them learn to pray more effectively. For example, a list for a college campus might include:

● pray for Christian campus ministries,

● pray for more Christian professors and administrative personnel,

● pray for students to build healthy friendships and other relationships,

● pray for drugs and alcohol to be replaced by God's love in students' lives,

● pray for students to avoid sexual relationships before marriage, and

● pray for students to embrace Jesus Christ instead of the false religions and philosophies so prevalent on college campuses.

Create a unique list of prayer ideas for each prayer walk kids go on. Also, plan the prayer route in advance so that the group ends up at a restaurant or some other fun location. Once you arrive, close your prayer time and give kids time to relax and rest their feet.

TIP BOX

One way to model prayer for your kids is to practice "on-the-spot" prayers in all your relationships. Every day we hear from friends and acquaintances about problems in their lives and personal issues they're struggling with. Rather than saying, "I'll be thinking about you" or "I'll pray for you this week," ask to pray for them on the spot. Simply say, "I can tell this is a real struggle for you. Can I pray for you about this?" If your friend says yes, just move off to a quiet spot and pray for a few minutes about the problem or issue.

This approach may feel awkward at first—that's OK. After a while it will seem quite natural. And once kids see you living out prayer as a priority in your life, they'll soon begin doing the same.

SMALL-GROUP PRAYER CLOSET

Many meeting rooms have storage closets or smaller adjacent rooms for kids to use. One valuable way to make prayer a strong focus of your small group is to convert a large storage closet or small meeting room into a prayer closet.

All you need to create a prayer closet is a small table, a few chairs, a Bible, and an "occupied" sign to hang on the door handle. If you want to add more detail to the room, consider decorating the walls with prayers from the Bible (for example, Psalm 139 or Ephesians 1:17-21) and lighting the room with a small table lamp. Also, you might include a pad and pen for kids to use to write out their prayers (see "Small-Group Prayer Journal" on page 95).

Once you've set up the room, dedicate it to be used only for prayer. Once kids understand the purpose of the room, tell them to feel free to use it whenever they want to be alone to pray or to pray with one or two other people.

Incorporate the prayer closet into your regular meeting times with kids by encouraging them to use the prayer room after meetings to pray for any special needs that came up during the evening.

TIP BOX

To make the prayer room more accessible to kids all the time, set up the room in a place that has outside access. Change the lock on the outside door and provide willing group members with keys. Place different locks on all the other doors inside the prayer room so kids won't have access to the rest of the church or home.

Before handing out keys to kids, lay down specific rules for how the prayer room may be used. If kids understand the true purpose of the prayer room, they'll be less likely to take it for granted.

SMALL-GROUP PRAYER JOURNAL

Purchase several large blank books for group members to use as group prayer journals. Set a journal in a prayer room or simply keep it available in the small-group meeting room. Encourage kids to write their prayers in the book whenever they wish. The only rule is that prayers must be dated and may not contain gossip or backbiting about specific individuals. Other than that, anything goes. Tell kids they don't have to include their names if they don't want to.

Take a journal on trips with the group, and provide times when individuals can use it to log their prayers. Encourage kids to read through past prayers to see how other people express themselves to God. Keep the journals as ongoing records of God's work in your group members' lives.

"My prayer is not for [the disciples] alone. I pray also for those who will believe in me through their message, that all of them may be one, Father, just as you are in me and I am in you. May they also be in us so that the world may believe that you have sent me. I have given them the glory that you gave me, that they may be one as we are one: I in them and you in me. May they be brought to complete unity to let the world know that you sent me and have loved them even as you have loved me."

—John 17:20-23

Let's set the scene.

It was just hours before Jesus' arrest—probably the most emotionally intense time of his life on earth. Jesus' personal anguish over what he was about to face was so profound that the Bible says, "His sweat was like drops of blood falling to the ground" (Luke 22:44). His concern wasn't only for his own life—the pain of his coming crucifixion and the far greater agony of taking the world's sin onto himself. It was also for his followers, who were soon to be like "scattered sheep" with no shepherd (Matthew 26:31).

In the hours before Jesus' death, Jesus and the disciples prayed one last time together. The focus of Jesus' prayer was unity—the unity of believers. Jesus could have prayed for many things—victory over sin, protection from harm, success in spreading the Gospel, purity in life, faithfulness to God—yet he chose to pray for unity.

Why unity?

Part of the answer may seem obvious. Unity inspires commitment, provides people with a place to belong, and creates an environment in which deeper, more vulnerable relationships can flourish. As a small-group leader, building group unity probably ranks as one of your highest goals. But is that the only reason Jesus prayed for us to have unity—so we could live together harmoniously and always have a place to belong?

No. Look closer: "May they be brought to complete unity *to let the world know that you sent me and have loved them* even as you have loved me." The New Century Version says it even more clearly: "I will be in them and you will be in me so that they will be completely one. *Then the world will know* that you sent me and that you loved them just as much as you loved me."

Jesus knew the deeper reason your small group needs unity. Beyond the internal benefits (which are wonderful), unity provides the *external* evidence that convinces the world that Jesus really was sent from God and that his love for us is real. Unity among Christians is a vital part of God's plan of salvation for the world.

No wonder unity was so important to Christ.

As small-group leaders, we too understand the importance of unity. We tend to struggle, however, when it comes to defining exactly what unity means and how it should be lived out in kids' lives.

The definition of unity in your small group changes

depending on the "mental model" you use in defining your group as a whole. For example, if a group is modeled after a business or an organization, then the unity of the group members will probably be defined by their adherence to a specific purpose or cause and their willingness to live by a set standard of behaviors that the leader defines. Likewise, if a group is seen as a type of social club, then unity may be measured by how similarly the members dress or talk, or by the fact that the group is the members' only social outlet.

These mental models may work well in some areas of life. But when it comes to the church—and to your small group—they simply aren't biblical. Nowhere in Scripture is the church defined as a business, an organization, or a social club. (By the way, that doesn't mean the church shouldn't be organized or social. It certainly should. But those are only aspects of a greater whole.)

Fortunately, the Bible does provide us with clear mental models we can use to define our small groups. They are a family and a body.

When you apply either of these models to your small group, unity suddenly takes on a drastically different meaning. For example, a family can be in unity even if nobody dresses the same, does the same things, or thinks the same way. Likewise, a body can function in perfect unity even though its various parts look and act quite differently from each other.

At its foundation, Christian unity isn't organizational. It's relational. That's why Paul wrote, "Bear with each other and forgive whatever grievances you may have against one another. Forgive as the Lord forgave you. And over all these virtues put on love, which binds them all together in perfect unity" (Colossians 3:13-14).

As a small-group leader, you'll determine what kind of unity your kids will build with each other. So throw away the business blueprints and the social-club agendas. Instead, focus your energy on building the deeper kind of unity God wants. As a small-group leader, you can help your kids forge deeper bonds of unity than they could in a larger group setting.

If you do, you'll not only be giving kids friendships that'll last a lifetime, but you'll also be showing the world around you the true evidence of Jesus and the reality of his love.

Use these ideas to help build true unity in your small group.

 BIRTHDAY BLESSINGS

Keep track of your group members' birthdays. Whenever a group member has a birthday, make it a part of your regular small-group meeting to give him or her a birthday blessing.

To give a birthday blessing, have kids form a circle around the birthday person. One at a time, have group members bless the birthday person in one of three ways:

● by telling one thing the birthday person has taught them about life in the past year,

● by telling one or more things they admire about the birthday person, or

● by telling one thing they wish for the birthday person in the coming year.

As each person shares, have the birthday person turn and face him or her. When everyone has shared, have group members huddle around and give the birthday person a group hug.

 CHURCH VISITATION

Unity involves the entire body of Christ. Encourage unity with your group members by taking them on a tour of services in other churches in your area. Visit all the major denominations, as well as some independent congregations.

After each visitation experience, ask:

● **What's your reaction to this church service?**

● **What did you think of the people we encountered?**

- **What surprised you about this service?**
- **What were some things you didn't understand?**
- **What questions does this experience raise about the way we worship God in our own church?**

TIP BOX
Keep track of the harder-to-answer questions kids have about the different churches they visit. Once you've collected several questions, invite your pastor to a small-group meeting to respond to them. (Be sure to give your pastor a copy of the questions in advance!)

CONFLICT-RESOLUTION RETREAT

Take kids on a retreat to learn how to "fight fair" and work through issues they may have with parents, God, or each other.

During the retreat, have kids role play the typical conflict situations they face, then discuss the best ways to work through those conflicts. Also play lots of competitive games, especially games that don't depend on physical prowess. After each game, debrief by asking kids to describe the nature of the conflict built into the game and how it's similar to or different from real-life conflict.

For the training part of the retreat, consider taking kids through the companion workbooks to *Caring Enough to Confront* or *Caring Enough to Hear & Be Heard,* both by David Augsburger (Herald Press).

TIP BOX
To build real unity in your group, you must model genuine vulnerability for your group members. As you stretch yourself and allow kids to see both the good and bad inside you, they'll learn how to be more vulnerable and trusting with each other.

DISCIPLE WALK

One of the ways Jesus built unity among the disciples was as easy as putting one foot in front of the other. They walked together a lot. You can re-create this simple yet effective way of building relationships among your group members.

Pick a pleasant day in the spring or fall for an "In His Steps" walk. Take kids on a walk between two towns (or two neighborhoods) in your area that are approximately seven miles apart, which is about the distance between Jerusalem and Emmaus (Luke 24:13-35). Encourage kids to interact on the journey by taking along and posing questions from a conversation-starter book.

Going on an extended walk with your group members is not only great exercise for them, but also can be an effective way to encourage them to interact and grow closer together.

LUNCH BUNCH

This simple idea is based on a principle carried out all through the Bible: Eating together is a bonding experience. Here are a couple ways you can help kids bond during the lunch hour.

● If kids all go to the same junior high or high school, join them in their cafeteria once a week for a shared meal.

● If kids go to various schools, start a Grazing Club during lunch on a certain day of the week. For example, have kids in the Grazing Club get together for a meal each Friday at a local hangout or every Sunday after church.

Whatever day you choose, make sure the Grazing Club always meets at the same time and at the same restaurant each week. That way kids who miss one week aren't left eating alone the next week when they show up at the wrong place.

MY FAVORITE EVENING

Have each group member write a description of an ideal night he or she would like to spend with a group of friends. Encourage kids to make sure their ideas aren't too expensive and can be done effectively with a small group.

Collect all the descriptions. Then, at random times during the year, have the whole group surprise one member by honoring him or her with that person's favorite evening.

As a memorial for the evening, present the honored guest with a card signed by each member of the group.

ROAMING SLUMBER PARTY

Each month (or every six weeks), sponsor an all-nighter at a different group member's home. Choose a different group of kids each time to plan the event and make it surprising and unique. Set only two rules for the group planning the event:

● Kids must provide a time for the group-member host to share his or her responses to the "All-Nighter Self-Disclosure Form" (p. 109).

● Kids must allow themselves at least six hours of sleep time.

Have group members bring sleeping bags, pillows, and whatever else they need to stay a night away from home. During the evening, gather kids around while the host member shares his or her responses to the handout.

ROCK BONDING

One great long-term way to build unity in your small group is to teach kids to rock climb together. Rock climbing requires kids to learn to trust each other in a fun and adventurous environment that's also good for their health.

Many health clubs and outdoor organizations offer half- or full-day classes for small groups, as well as guided full-day expeditions to go "bouldering" or rock climbing. Once kids are equipped and trained, take them out for a climb. Encourage climbing partners to trade off frequently so several different individuals get the chance to work together.

After the climb, gather kids together and ask:
● **What did you learn about rock climbing today?**
● **What did you learn about yourself today?**
● **What did you learn about other members of the group today?**

- **What lessons about unity and trust have you learned from this experience?**
- **What's one way today's experience might affect the way you relate to other members of the group? to other people in general?**

Because rock climbing is such a valuable "lesson-learning" sport, take kids out often for climbing expeditions. Each time, your group members will come away with new insights about themselves, each other, God, and the world around them.

 # SECRET SERVICE-PROJECTS

Brainstorm with group members a list of "random acts of kindness" for kids to work together on and perform in their church, a neighboring church, their neighborhoods, or your community. The acts of kindness can be anything from sweeping walks to baking cakes, but they must all be acts that can be done with absolute secrecy so no one knows your group was the culprit.

Once kids have created a list of possibilities, have them work together to make each act of kindness into a secret adventure. For example, if one act of kindness is to shovel snow off the walks in the neighborhood around the church, kids must find a way to do that without anyone seeing them or recognizing who they are.

For added fun, have group members leave an unsigned note that says something like "This random act of kindness was done for you as an effort to brighten your day and show you God's love. Have a great day!"

Encourage kids to challenge themselves with acts that may be particularly difficult to conceal (for example, giving people flowers or cleaning up a local park).

THIS IS MY STORY

Every few weeks ask a different group member to tell the whole group one thing he or she has learned about God recently. After the person shares, have the whole group stand and give him or her a standing ovation.

TIP BOX

For a fun combination, consider linking this idea with the "Person of the Week" idea on page 90. During your first week, assign one person to be the person of the week. At the next small-group meeting one week later, have that person share a faith story and receive a standing ovation. Then assign a new group member to be the next person of the week. That way at least two people will receive a special affirmation each week!

 # "THIS IS YOUR LIFE" COLLAGE

Have your group members create an "identity" collage to give to each group member on his or her birthday. All you need is a large piece of poster board, scissors, glue, and a stack of magazines. Have kids search through the magazines for images or words that convey something about the birthday person and cut those out of the magazines. For example, if your birthday person is a cowboy or cowgirl type, kids might find pictures of boots or a horse, or use magazine letters to spell out phrases such as "Round Up Another Year" or "Ride On!"

Once kids have chosen images and words, have them work together to compose a collage on the poster board. Then have group members present their birthday collage as a way of saying, "We love you" and "We're glad you're you."

SMALL-GROUP COMMUNION

In addition to your church's regular congregational communion time, share communion with your small-group members on a regular basis. Each time you take communion with your kids, vary your format. For example, you can have communion

- around candle-lit circular tables,
- outside under the stars,
- with adults serving the communion to kids,
- with young people from a sister church, or
- combined with an extended group-singing time.

If your faith tradition requires an ordained pastor to administer the communion, ask the pastor to join with you in planning the various communion services, then participate with your group in each one.

Provide time for group members to pray together for one another's needs, as well as a time for personal silent reflection.

SMALL-GROUP MISSION STATEMENT

One effective way to build unity in your small group is to have kids work together to create a unified mission statement. There are many ways to do this. One way is to have kids brainstorm several answers to this question: "What do you want this small group to be remembered for after we've all gone our separate ways?"

Use kids' responses as the basis for formulating their group mission statement. Also encourage young people to support their statement with appropriate Bible verses. It may take a few meetings to complete the statement. Once the statement is complete, post it everywhere in your church and provide kids with small framed editions to place in their bedrooms at home.

Remind kids of the mission statement often. Encourage them to use it when they make decisions about how they're going to treat anyone who comes in contact with the group, including each other.

ALL-NIGHTER SELF-DISCLOSURE FORM

1. What's your full name?

2. Where and when were you born?

3. Who else is in your family?

4. How would you describe each of your family members in one sentence?

5. What was your favorite thing to do as a child?

6. What's your favorite color?

7. What do you like to do when you have free time?

8. What's one of your pet peeves?

9. How would you describe yourself to someone who doesn't know you?

10. What's one fact about you that nobody in the room knows?

11. What's one dream you want to accomplish in your life-time?

12. What's one thing you like most about being a part of this group?

CHAPTER 9

ENCOURAGING
OTHERS
ONE TO ONE

"When Jesus saw Nathanael approaching, he said of him, 'Here is a true Israelite, in whom there is nothing false.' 'How do you know me?' Nathanael asked. Jesus answered, 'I saw you while you were still under the fig tree before Philip called you.' Then Nathanael declared, 'Rabbi, you are the Son of God; you are the King of Israel.' Jesus said, 'You believe because I told you I saw you under the fig tree? You shall see greater things than that.' "

—John 1:47-50

Jesus loved the multitudes, but his heart was always with the "one." His love and compassion compelled him to see beyond the mass of faces that passed him and to look into the eyes of the individual. It was Jesus' passion for the one that caused him to notice when one woman, among hundreds pressing against him, touched him and was healed (Luke 8:43-48). It was his passion for the one that caused him to stop as he walked among a crowd toward Jerusalem and notice a lone outcast perched in a tree (Luke 19:1-10). And it was that same passion that allowed him to see the beauty of Nathanael's heart, even before they had met face to face.

In a culture where the numbers game of big business too often invades the church, and youth workers' reputations are often ranked by the number of kids on their rosters, it's easy to forget that our Savior changed the world, not with armies but with a small group of twelve men. It's easy to gloss over the fact that Jesus *could've* raised an army of followers if he'd wanted to. He could've had twelve thousand apostles instead of twelve. But he didn't. Jesus knew that if he wanted to change the world, he wouldn't do it by amassing superior numbers. He would do it by changing one heart at a time. Jesus chose to reach the one. So he poured his heart into a handful of individuals who later went on to reshape the world.

Alone, the disciples were hardly extraordinary. In fact, by today's standards many would be considered uneducated, lower class citizens. But they were able to turn the world on its ear because of the extraordinary investment Jesus made in each of them—one to one.

Like Jesus, you are also the leader of a small group. Some of your kids may seem extraordinary to you, but many are probably like the disciples. And like Jesus, you have the opportunity to invest in your group members' lives one to one. With a small group, you can afford to expend the extra energy required to approach each young person as an individual and discover how to best reach that person with God's love and encouragement.

Leading a small group in this way requires a lot from you—but never at the expense of your own private life or family time. You must commit yourself to *each* group member's success. That means learning each young person's unique personality—understanding his or her strengths and weaknesses—and investing in that person for the sole purpose of seeing him or her succeed in Christ. It also means allowing kids to see you for who you really are—at your best and your worst.

There's no guarantee about how kids will respond to you. Some may love you for caring; a few may reject you and even laugh at your weaknesses. Still others may be indifferent to any amount of love you show. But some will be transformed by the love of God working through you—and later go on to change the world.

GROUP-APPLICATION IDEAS

Use these ideas to deepen your one-to-one relationships with your small-group members.

BOOKWORMS

Ask individuals in your group what kind of books they like to read or what Bible books or subjects they'd like to know more about. If you discover you have similar interests, ask each person if you can read (or study) a particular book together.

If it's a fiction book, simply buy two copies and read it at the same time as your group member. Then talk about how the characters are like or unlike people you know in real life.

If the book you choose is a nonfiction book or a book of the Bible, read one chapter each week, then get together to discuss it. As a help to your partner, come up with challenging questions based on the text that you know apply to his or her life.

Use the book as a basis to get to know each other better. Share with your partner how what you learn in the book affects your attitudes and actions, and come up with ways that

TIP BOX

If you're looking for thought-provoking novels to read together, consider classics such as *The Chronicles of Narnia* by C.S. Lewis, *In His Steps* by Charles Sheldon, or *The Divine Romance* by Gene Edwards. Also check out your local Christian bookstore for a rapidly growing collection of new Christian novels.

If you're interested in exploring some of the classic secular novels on the market, check out the *Lord of the Rings* trilogy by J.R.R. Tolkien or even *Moby Dick* by Herman Melville.

you can help each other make the changes that the book inspires.

CHEERING SECTION

At the beginning of each school year, give kids copies of the "In-Your-Corner Survey" (p. 115), and have kids fill them out. Allow kids one week to provide you with the information the survey asks for.

Once you have all the completed surveys, mark on your calendar important dates in your kids' lives; for example, sports competitions, speech or drama contests, or rodeo and livestock competitions. Make it a point not to schedule any small-group events at those times and to clear your own schedule so you can attend events for each group member. Also, update these forms throughout the year as kids learn more about their schedules.

COFFEE NIGHT

At least once every six months, spend an evening in a coffee shop or another relaxed setting with just one member of your group. Set no agenda other than to spend time together talking.

TIP BOX
When spending one-on-one time with group members of the opposite sex, it's important to invite another adult friend along so your group member won't feel uncomfortable or get the wrong idea about your time together.

To help keep the conversation going, memorize a list of open-ended questions that directly relate to the young person's life. For example, "Scott, you've only lived in Burgersmerger for about six months. How has it been for you finding new friends?" or "I understand you're in the band. Why did you decide to commit the time to join up?"

After each meeting, take a few minutes to jot down the major points of

SMALL-GROUP **BODY BUILDERS**

IN-YOUR-CORNER SURVEY

Name _____

School _____

Grade _____

Phone _____

What sports teams, music groups, or other extracurricular organizations are you involved with this year?

Please attach to this survey copies of all the schedule information for your extracurricular activities in the coming year (such as game schedules, practice schedules, contest schedules, or production schedules). I will use this information as a guide for planning the events for our group this year. Thanks!

the conversation, as well as any insights you gained about the young person. Keep this information in a log you can refer to as a reminder to pray and stay current in kids' lives.

HANG-OUT NIGHT

Schedule one night each week as a "hang-out night" at your home. If you have no regular service on Sunday evenings, that time might work best. Plan nothing for the evening, and make sure kids understand it's not your job to entertain them in your home. Explain that you're opening your home to provide kids with a peaceful place to hang out and to let them see you in your element.

When kids come over, encourage them to make themselves at home. Watch television with them, play a game of chess or Pente, or just sit and talk awhile. It's a great way to get to know each other outside the more programmed environment of church activities.

TIP BOX

As a safety precaution for yourself and others, set up a rule that no kids of the opposite sex can hang out at your place unless they bring along a friend of their own. It's better to avoid situations that might make you or others feel uncomfortable.

JOINT PROJECTS

Make it your personal goal to discover at least one common interest you have with each young person in your group. Once you have found these common interests, set up a series of joint projects you can do with various group members throughout the year.

Here are a few projects that work well with a partner:

- playing basketball
- working on cars
- rock climbing
- decorating shirts
- playing guitar
- sewing or stitchery work
- silk-screening
- running

- building model rockets
- writing and reading poetry
- doing volunteer work
- shopping

- playing racquetball
- hiking
- fishing
- cooking

PRIVATE BIRTHDAY DESSERT

Keep track of group members' birthdays; then when each person's special day comes around, take the birthday person out for a dessert treat "on the house." During your time together, tell the birthday person how you've seen him or her grow in the past year.

PRIVATE JOURNALS

Keep a separate journal of prayers and encouragement for each young person in your group. Write a page or so in each journal every few weeks, dating each entry to help keep track of your writing schedule. Include messages of encouragement, praises for past successes, hopes for the future, and written prayers for each person.

Give the journals to kids as special gifts each Christmas.

TIP BOX
As a creative way to combine two ideas, consider merging this journal with the "Prayer Record" idea (p. 91). Simply separate the journal into two sections—one for letters and one for the prayer record. Date all your entries so kids can see how you've prayed for them over the past year and what you've written to them as encouragement.

SCHOLARSHIP ADVOCATE

One powerful way to develop one-to-one relationships with group members is to demonstrate your personal commitment to each group member's success. One way to do this is to act as a scholarship advocate for kids about to graduate from high school.

Make it your business to learn about the many scholarships and grants available to kids entering college. Gather all the information you can from the counselor at your local high school and from scholarship organizations.

Once you have the information, study it to see which scholarships might work well for any of your group members who are about to graduate. Meet with each of your juniors and seniors to discuss their scholarship options. Assist kids in filling out the proper forms and sending them off to various colleges and organizations.

SELF-MADE GIFTS

If you're artistic, consider making an Easter gift for each of your group members every year. Choose a gift that's inexpensive and easy to create yet can be personalized for each person. For example, you could use a calligraphy set to write out and frame a special verse for each young person in your group. Or you could use wood and leather to create rustic crosses with a special phrase carved in the wood, such as "J. C. Loves (kid's initials)."

Deliver the gifts to kids' homes on Sunday afternoon. Include a simple card wishing each group member a happy Easter.

TEAM LEADING

A good way to build relationships with individuals in your group is to let them act as your co-leaders during your small-group meetings.

Every six or seven weeks, ask a different young person to act as your co-leader in your group's weekly meetings. To the degree that the person feels comfortable, have him or her lead various parts of the meeting and assist you with certain activities.

Each week increase the responsibility level of your co-leader until by the final week, he or she is leading most or all of the meeting, with you acting as the assistant.

Here's a sample schedule of how this process might work:

● Week 1—You lead everything, with co-leader acting as your assistant on one or two activities.

● Week 2—Co-leader gives the announcements and assists you with one or two activities.

● Week 3—Co-leader does the opening activity, reads the announcements, and assists you with a few more activities.

● Week 4—Co-leader does the opening activity, announcements, and one additional activity.

● Week 5—Co-leader does the opening, reads the announcements, and leads the primary discussion time. You act as his or her assistant when you're not leading.

● Week 6—Co-leader does everything except the closing, with you acting as his or her assistant.

● Week 7—Co-leader leads everything, with you acting as his or her assistant.

Spend time with your co-leaders, helping them develop leadership skills and praising them as they grow in confidence and maturity. At the end of your time together, treat your co-leader to a free breakfast at your favorite local restaurant.

BUILDING MENTORING RELATIONSHIPS

Using the activities and ideas suggested in this chapter is a great way to build deeper one-to-one relationships with kids. To make your bonds with group members even stronger, consider these underlying guidelines for building healthy mentoring relationships.

1. Show, don't tell. Avoid telling kids what they should or shouldn't do in the various situations they face. Offer advice only when they ask for it or when you believe the consequences of their choices may be dangerous. Instead of telling kids what they should do, show them what they should do by letting them see the way you live. That way, when they do ask your opinion, your words will carry a great deal more weight.

2. Learn from your students. Humble yourself with your kids by looking for ways they can teach you. For example, one group member might be able to teach you about fishing or about a sport you'd like to play. Another may be able to help you with your car or even show you how to sew your own clothes. Finding things kids can teach you helps them feel more valued in the relationship and actually causes them to esteem you more.

3. Respect each other. Never talk about your group members' problems with others who aren't already involved. Never speak negatively about your kids to anyone. Always speak about your kids with the highest regard for their personal honor. By doing this, kids will see that you're trustworthy and that you have integrity.

4. Reveal your weaknesses. When kids ask how you're doing, share your real struggles with them. To avoid betraying confidences with your spouse, family, church members, or close friends, focus on personal struggles you're having with God or with yourself. Kids want to know you're human too, so they can feel free to share their own struggles.

5. Act as a mirror. Don't be afraid to tell kids what you see when you look at their lives. Most kids are eager for someone they respect to help them figure out who they really are. If kids know you love them, they'll appreciate your honesty. Make an effort to reflect to kids what they present to the world so they can know how their choices may be affecting others.

6. Seek out challenges. Design spiritual projects for your kids that stretch them to grow in their relationships with God. For example, if one person has a hard time spending time alone, challenge him or her to spend one evening with no one else around, then write about his or her reactions. If someone has a hard time reaching out to others, ask him or her to accompany you to a homeless shelter or to a hospital for a visit with patients.

7. Balance "light" and "heavy" times. If all your conversations with kids are heavy, they may begin to dread your times together simply because those times take so much emotional energy. Avoid this by planning fun times between the deep talks. See a movie together, play a game, or just talk. This will also help dispel the myth that you live on an exalted spiritual plane.

8. Stay healthy. Sometimes kids may take advantage of your relationship because they think it's your job to like them and spend time with them. Avoid this unhealthy situation by maintaining honest connections with kids. If they offend you, tell them. If they take advantage of you, confront them. Kids will be more than willing to respond positively to your honesty. However, if a young person takes advantage of you repeatedly after being confronted, warn him or her that your relationship is in danger because of the choices he or she has made. If the person still doesn't change, gently break off the relationship.

ONE-TO-ONE RELATIONAL PLANNER

Use this planner to better organize your time with each of the people in your small group.

GROUP MEMBER	ACTIVITY DATES AND DESCRIPTIONS
Name: _____	Coffee Night _____
Birthday: _____	_____
Phone: _____	_____
Interests: _____	_____
_____	Joint Projects _____
_____	_____
_____	_____
_____	_____
_____	Activities I've Attended _____
_____	_____
_____	_____
_____	_____
_____	_____
_____	Easter Gift Ideas _____
_____	_____
_____	_____
_____	_____
_____	_____
_____	_____
_____	_____
_____	Birthday Desserts _____
_____	_____
_____	_____
_____	_____
_____	_____
_____	Team Leading_____
_____	_____
_____	_____
_____	_____
_____	_____

Group Publishing, Inc.
Attention: Books & Curriculum
P.O. Box 481
Loveland, CO 80539
Fax: (970) 669-1994

Evaluation for *Small-Group Body Builders*

Please help Group Publishing, Inc., continue to provide innovative and useful resources for ministry. Please take a moment to fill out this evaluation and mail or fax it to us. Thanks!

● ● ●

1. As a whole, this book has been (circle one)

not very helpful   very helpful

1   2   3   4   5   6   7   8   9   10

2. The best things about this book:

3. Ways this book could be improved:

4. Things I will change because of this book:

5. Other books I'd like to see Group publish in the future:

6. Would you be interested in field-testing future Group products and giving us your feedback? If so, please fill in the information below:

Name _____

Street Address _____

City _____ State _____ Zip _____

Phone Number _____ Date _____

Bible Study Series

Give Your Teenagers a Solid Faith Foundation That Lasts a Lifetime!

Here are the *essentials* of the Christian life—core values teenagers *must* believe to make good decisions now...and build an *unshakable* lifelong faith. Developed by youth workers like you...field-tested with *real* youth groups in *real* churches...here's the meat your kids *must* have to grow spiritually—presented in a fun, involving way!

Each 4-session **Core Belief Bible Study Series** book lets you easily...

- Lead deep, compelling, *relevant* discussions your kids won't want to miss...
- Involve teenagers in exploring life-changing truths...
- Help kids create healthy relationships with each other—and you!
- **Plus you'll make an *eternal difference* in the lives of your kids** as you give them a solid faith foundation that stands firm on God's Word.

Here are the Core Belief Bible Study Series titles already available...

Senior High Studies

Why **Being a Christian** Matters	0-7644-0883-6	Why **Spiritual Growth** Matters	0-7644-0884-4
Why **Creation** Matters	0-7644-0880-1	Why **Suffering** Matters	0-7644-0879-8
Why **Forgiveness** Matters	0-7644-0887-9	Why **the Bible** Matters	0-7644-0882-8
Why **God** Matters	0-7644-0874-7	Why **the Church** Matters	0-7644-0890-9
Why **God's Justice** Matters	0-7644-0886-0	Why **the Holy Spirit** Matters	0-7644-0876-3
Why **Jesus Christ** Matters	0-7644-0875-5	Why **the Last Days** Matter	0-7644-0888-7
Why **Love** Matters	0-7644-0889-5	Why **the Spiritual Realm** Matters	0-7644-0881-X
Why **Personal Character** Matters	0-7644-0885-2		

Junior High/Middle School Studies

The Truth About **Being a Christian**	0-7644-0859-3	The Truth About **Sin and Forgiveness**	0-7644-0863-1
The Truth About **Creation**	0-7644-0856-9	The Truth About **Spiritual Growth**	0-7644-0860-7
The Truth About **Developing Character**	0-7644-0861-5	The Truth About **Suffering**	0-7644-0855-0
		The Truth About **the Bible**	0-7644-0858-5
The Truth About **God**	0-7644-0850-X	The Truth About **the Church**	0-7644-0899-2
The Truth About **God's Justice**	0-7644-0862-3	The Truth About **the Holy Spirit**	0-7644-0852-6
The Truth About **Jesus Christ**	0-7644-0851-8	The Truth About **the Last Days**	0-7644-0864-X
The Truth About **Love**	0-7644-0865-8	The Truth About **the Spiritual Realm**	0-7644-0857-7

Practical Resources for Your Youth Ministry

PointMaker™ Devotions for Youth Ministry

Here's active learning at its best—with 45 PointMakers™ that will help your teenagers discover, understand, and apply biblical principles. PointMakers work on their own for brief meetings on specific topics or slide easily into any youth curriculum to make a lasting impression. They're devotions with an attitude—getting your kids up and involved! **Included:** handy Scripture and topical indexes that make it quick and easy to select the perfect PointMaker for any lesson you want to teach!

ISBN 0-7644-2003-8

Quick Help!

Here are the practical solutions you've looked for to your most perplexing youth ministry problems—from ministry pros! You'll learn how to recruit and hang on to excellent volunteers...work with even unreasonable parents...balance professional and personal lives...get through to youth in ways that matter...and discover outreach ideas that *work*. BONUS: exhaustive table of contents organizes ideas by topics, so ideas are always at your fingertips!

ISBN 0-7644-2018-6

Youth Worker's Idea Depot™

Here are Group's 1,001 greatest ideas for youth ministry—on one convenient CD-ROM! Practical, proven ideas gathered from front-line ministry professionals make this a *gold mine* of ministry solutions! Save time! You can search these ideas instantly—by Scripture...topic...key words...or by personal notes you've entered into your database. And you can add your new ideas at any time! Save money! You'll get a complete library of ideas—plus a trial subscription to Group Magazine, where you'll discover dozens of new ideas in every issue!

Categories of ideas on your **Idea Depot** disk include: learning games, creative readings, adventures, object lessons, skits, retreats and overnighters, devotions, projects, affirmation activities, creative prayers, music ideas, creative Bible studies, and parties!

ISBN 0-7644-2034-8

Worship Ideas for Youth Ministry

Get your teenagers excited about worship—*and* about God! Each worship idea is based on a passage from the Gospels. Ideas include traditional forms of worship and exciting new ideas—perfect for starting youth meetings, developing a biblical theme, enjoying a special youth worship and prayer meeting...or helping youth lead an entire congregation in worship. If you're a youth worker, event leader, Christian club or camp director, or Christian school teacher, you'll use this collection of relevant, easy-prep worship experiences again and again!

ISBN 0-7644-2002-X

Order today from your local Christian bookstore, or write:
Group Publishing, P.O. Box 485, Loveland, CO 80539.

It's a party...a Bible adventure...and a dress-up event— all rolled into one!

Here's a brand-new way to get teenagers (and adults) involved in Bible learning! They'll act out roles as they play fun games, and discover new insights into important Bible stories! Each game comes with complete instructions to design an event that lasts three hours...or three days...it's up to you!

Included: event invitations, character descriptions, decorating tips, clues, costuming ideas, menus, advertising clip art, Bible-application ideas, and a step-by-step planning guide.

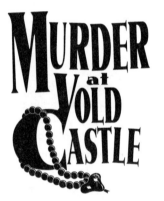

Robert & Linda Klimek

Visitors to this historic fortress discover their host, Baron von Schnell, has been killed...and every guest is a suspect! As your kids act out their roles, they'll experience the same intrigues and conflicts lived out by Saul and David—and prepare for an exciting Bible study.

ISBN 1-55945-694-9

THE CASE OF THE MISSING PROFESSOR

Robert & Linda Klimek

Not much happens in Wallar Hollar... except that the professor has disappeared! Somebody knows more than he or she is saying—but who? This down-home experience raises the same fear... confusion...joy...and surprise experienced by men and women who knew Jesus.

ISBN 1-55945-776-7